PAVEMENT FOR MY PILLOW

CHRIS KITCH

PAVEMENT FOR MY PILLOW

*A Homeless Woman's
Climb from
Degradation to Dignity*

With a Foreword by
ROBIN WATERFIELD

 HAZELDEN®

INFORMATION & EDUCATIONAL SERVICES

Hazelden
Center City, Minnesota 55012-0176
1-800-328-0094
1-651-257-1331 (fax)
www.hazelden.org

The right of Chris Kitch to be identified as the author of this work has been asserted by her in accordance with the Copyright, Designs and Patents Act 1988.

First published in Great Britain in 1996 by Orion
An imprint of Orion Books Ltd.
Orion House, 5 Upper St. Martin's Lane, London WC2H 9EA
(Originally titled *Pavement for My Pillow: The Astonishing Story of
One Woman's Climb from Pitiful Baglady to Scholar and Writer*)

First American edition published in 1998 by The Hazelden Foundation by arrangement with Orion Books Ltd. Printed in the United States of America. No portion of this publication may be reproduced in any manner without the written permission of the publisher.

A CIP catalogue record for this book is available from the British Library.

Library of Congress Cataloging-in-Publication Data
Kitch, Chris. 1938–
    Pavement for my pillow : a homeless woman's climb from degradation
to dignity / Chris Kitch.
        p.   cm.
    Originally published: London : Orion Books, 1996.
    ISBN 1-56838-191-3
    1. Homeless women—Great Britain—Biography.   I. Title.
HV4545.A4K57   1998
305.569′092—dc21
    [B]   98-22418
                                                                          CIP

01 00 99 98   6 5 4 3 2 1

Book design by Will Powers
Typesetting by Stanton Publication Services, Inc.
Cover design by David Spohn

CONTENTS

FOREWORD

by Robin Waterfield

My association with the remarkable author of this remarkable book came about through the kindness of another remarkable woman, Sister Frances Dominica of All Saints, Sisters of the Poor, through whose vision and persistence Helen House, the first hospice for children with life-threatening illnesses, came into existence.

The sisters had given my wife and me friendship and a place to live some years before this, and we were part of what they called their extended community. Another beneficiary of their friendship and support was Chris Kitch.

After the successful showing of the television program *Raising Lazarus,* based on her life, it was inevitable that the writing of an autobiography should be undertaken. But how to go about it? Since I had a background in publishing and had written a little myself, I was an obvious choice to help Chris.

When we set out to consider the project, I was immediately impressed by Chris's wonderful ability to recall and relate her experiences in a vivid narrative form. We decided that the best way to proceed was to sit with a tape recorder between us and have Chris tell me the story of her life.

I do not think either of us realized at the beginning what an enormous emotional experience this exercise would be. Chris's life had plumbed the depths of shame and degradation but also had reached unimagined heights of achievement and joy. For both of us, it will remain an unforgettable experience. I can only testify to the courage and endurance shown by Chris in completing this task. I believe the end product, which is this book, *Pavement for My Pillow,* will speak to many and will give new hope and encouragement to all who read it.

ACKNOWLEDGMENTS

This story was written from my heart. I needed special help to get it down in print. Amanda White, my editor, provided that special something that makes a story into a book. Her unswerving belief in the value of this story helped me sustain my belief. Serafina Clarke, my agent, provided support and straight speaking, and she and Yvette Goulden at Orion Publishing held fast to their belief in me. Thank you. To Robin Waterfield, my "minder," who was enthusiastic with me, was excited for me, and spent hours listening to me. He is an octogenarian and gave to me much of his greatest gift—his time. You have my deepest gratitude. To Sophie also, thank you for your generosity and hospitality in welcoming me into your and Robin's home. To Caius Julyan, the director of *Raising Lazarus,* which told my life story as a documentary. Thank you for opening this door for me. I will never forget. To Mother Helen and Sister Frances Dominica for the sheer breadth of their understanding and support; my friends in the kitchen and St. John's Home, not forgetting the Porch and Helen House workers. To all those in the community of All Saints, Oxford, who have wished me well. Many thanks are due.

The University of North London provided the venue for making my childhood dream a reality. My thanks to the first full-time group of women who took the women's studies program I was privileged to study. I was inspired by the commitment of many women, particularly Dr. Lucy Bland, Dr. Helen Crowley, Professor Sue Lees (women's studies), Dr. Wendy Wheeler, Dr. Clare Buck (English literature), and Pat Jackson. These women encouraged me; they knew instinctively my love of learning. To Dr. Merle Collins (Caribbean studies), from whom I learned so much about dignity and politics. Thank you. There are too many to mention them all individually, but thank you, Milton, for all those brilliant games of table tennis, and Sheila McElliglot and Jenny Dale; how could I ever forget your warmth and friendship? Many heartfelt thanks to Jennifer McCabe and Prue Stevenson, director and former director of WISH (Women in Special Hospitals) who have given practical and emotional support to me; the management committee, particularly Susan Raven for her humor, kindness, and lifts to the Oxford coach after meetings. To Lesley Hayes, my counselor at the Libra Project, for her invaluable support. Many thanks.

To Linda Joffé for her supportive articles. To the M.A. full-time group at Oxford Brookes 1995–1996, in particular Caroline Jackson Houlston and Professor Mary Chamberlain, not forgetting the staff in the administration office for their tremendous support. To all those people who have written to me or spoken to me in the street or in the gym or in the shops where they worked. Thank you for your support. For the financial support I have received from so many people, thank you. To all those women and men, many insisting on anonymity, who have given me so much. I believe that it is in the living of my life that my gratitude speaks. Telling my story is but a small way of expressing a gratitude for which there is no language.

I

THE SINS OF THE FATHERS

1

BASTARD

Oxford, 19 June 1995. This morning I took my dogs, Bess, Bella, and Dancer, down to Meadow Lane by the river. They played wildly. Dancer, a whippet crossed with a Pharaoh hound, so graceful in movement, leaped and ran swiftly. Bella, a small white Staffordshire bull-terrier crossed with a Jack Russell, has two black markings over her eyes almost like shades. Bess, an Irish terrier dumped on the A40 as a puppy, has become Bella's foster mother; a reddish ginger in color, sturdy, swift, and extremely rebellious, she shakes her hips like a dancer.

Sitting in the remaining part of a rotting tree trunk, I watched the traffic on the water. At 7:30 A.M. it was very busy. There were several tourists in punts, taking in a scene more fitting to a nineteenth-century novel. Women students, eight to a boat, were rowing at an Olympic speed, coaxed by coxswains in preparation for the highlight of the year, the intercollege rowing championship. Glancing up, I thought that the blue of the Oxford sky was such a special shade, and the sun shone, warming me.

We live, the four of us, in a flat in the grounds of All Saints Convent. All Saints is a rambling house built of Cotswold stone. It houses twenty-one sisters and St. John's, a residential home for the elderly. The convent is on several acres of beautiful gardens, lawns, and an orchard and is just off Cowley Road in Oxford East. Helen House, the first hospice for children, founded by Sister Frances Dominica, is also on the convent grounds. A chapel built of the same Cotswold stone with wonderful windows depicting saints and martyrs captures my gaze whenever I stroll on the grounds. There is a hostel and a house in which I have a flat. The Porch, a drop-in center for hungry, homeless, or needy people, opens twice daily.

Down there by the river, with its thicket-covered meadow, it is hard to realize the city center is but a few minutes' walk away. Oxford is the city where I began my recovery from drug addiction. It has a dignity that emanates from its historical buildings. In Oxford's doorways and alleys, people sit and beg—drunk, drugged, forlorn, and forgotten people. They are society's "problems," the scapegoats here as elsewhere for a society that pretends but does not really practice care—but a society that I think wants to care. Oxford's spires call me to do more than worship their beauty. I both walk and speak in Oxford's colleges. The High Street is often filled with men and women dressed in caps and gowns, collecting their degree awards. There is a town crier, ringing his bell and announcing some product for sale; a gorilla holding a board that says, "Jeans £34 per pair"; a modern-day organ grinder playing his instant music, his act filled with characters for the children. There are beautiful grounds and gardens in all the colleges. How could people not learn here?

As my dogs and I return to the convent, I make a connection between the place of my birth and the passionate, hungry interest I have in religion. I feel my war is over and my horror has passed. My wounds are healing. And now I can begin to reflect on my life.

I was born at St. Monica's Home, Bellevue, near Manningham Lane, Bradford, Yorkshire, on 24 May 1938. Close by was an army barracks. St. Monica's Home was a place for the children of unwed mothers. My mother was in service as a maid and came to visit me at St. Monica's. I don't remember whether she lived there.

When recalling my first conscious memory, I see myself as a girl child with golden-blond hair and large brown eyes. This little girl is excited, jumping up and down in a high chair. In one hand she holds a spotted toy dog. The source of her pleasure is a woman dressed in a smart skirt and jacket with a striped blouse underneath. Her hair is lightly permed. She is the little girl's mother. The mother returns the greeting. She is wearing glasses, which she takes off and wipes.

My next vivid memory is of the same girl child, between eighteen months and two years old. In the high chair, she waits excited and eager, but her face crumples as her mother arrives, linking the arm of a man in uniform. This time there is no spontaneity. The mother is nervous and unsure. The man frightens the child, and she instinctively knows that her relationship with her mother has changed. She knows that it is because of this man.

These two experiences dominate the memories of my stay at St. Monica's. I have no recollection of how it looked or anyone else who was there, only vague stirrings that it was a place run by religious people.

My mother was born in 1908 in Castleford, Yorkshire, the eldest of four children. Her father, Herbert Kitching, had been a soldier under Lord Kitchener in World War I. Her mother, Florence Rachel Louise Hugo, came from Windsor, and became Mrs. Kitching. My mother had bad eyesight, which went untreated due to lack of money. At age twelve or thirteen, she went into service while her sister Laura became a weaver in the woolen industry.

I was born in 1938, the result of a "brief encounter." In 1940 my mother married George Wilkinson, the man she had brought to St. Monica's, the man who had filled me with so much fear in my early memory.

George Wilkinson had fought in World War II and had been wounded in his left thigh. A woman named Margaret, whom he had loved, was killed in the Blitz. George was born in Wigan, Lancashire, on 23 September 1896. He worked as an engineer's laborer. Just under six feet tall with broad shoulders and a military way of walking, he had grayish blue eyes, cropped hair, and yellowish skin that fitted tightly over his cheekbones. He looked to me like a Japanese man. With chest problems and a hernia, he was ill much of his time.

I moved with my mother in 1941 from St. Monica's to a tree-lined street in the Great Horton district of Bradford—42 Ash Grove—where she gave birth to a boy she named Trevor. He had big brown eyes and golden curls. My mother was intelligent with a biting wit; she was also pleasant and amusing. I loved her soprano voice. She sang much of the time and taught me about music, and she loved to read romances. My mother cooked, cleaned, and eventually was able to make a home for her family—she had learned the role of servant well, unpaid as a wife.

As a child, I spent a lot of time out on my own. I remember soldiers being friendly to me and giving me coins. I used to say hello to them and hold my hand out. The soldiers were in uniform; they spoke a funny language and held things called rifles in their hands. I think they were Belgian, and the money they gave me could not be spent in English shops.

Later we moved to Richmond Road, a street with cobblestones, no trees, and some derelict houses. We lived in one room. My stepfather was back in the army then, and sometimes he visited. On one of his visits, when I was four years old, something nasty happened to me. I think my grandmother had died, and we went to visit my grandfather. He lived in a house in Castleford—an industrial town in the West Riding of Yorkshire—where my mother had grown up. Here also lived her blond-haired brother Arnold, who had a wandering eye but was still considered good-looking. During this visit, while my mother was upstairs with her father, my Uncle Arnold pulled me between his legs. Turning my back to him, he pressed something against me, and with his hands he went inside my knickers and touched me. He whispered, "This is our secret." As footsteps sounded on the stairs, he stopped what he was doing.

The next day we visited again, and this time my stepfather was with us. I ran to my uncle—he was my new friend—but he wasn't too pleased to see me. We shared a secret, but he said in front of everyone that he didn't like me.

I replied, "I don't like you either."

My only memories of that time relate to Arnold Kitching, child abuser. I saw him once more when he stayed overnight and slept in the double bed with my mother in my stepfather's bedroom, while my stepfather was working nights at Croft's engineering factory in Thornbury, a district in Bradford. There was something strange going on that I didn't like. I was told not to mention that Arnold had stayed.

We moved to Tumbling Hill Street when I was six years old, and it became the street of my childhood. An even poorer place than Richmond Road, number 121 was our first house. It had two bedrooms, a cellar, an attic, and a living room. We rented it because nobody else wanted to live there. Some of the houses on that street were almost derelict and seemed to lean on each other for support. They had slate roofs and tall chimneys. The street was cobblestoned, and the milkman's and coalman's arrivals were always heralded by the sound of their horses' shoes striking sharply on the cobbles. No trees graced this street; instead, gas lamps stood like dark beacons waiting to be lit. They would wait until the war ended.

Food was rationed, too, and each family had ration books as well as identity cards. In spite of my mother's insistence that she had married George Wilkinson to give me a name, I hadn't gotten it—she had. The name on my book and card was different from the family name. Mine was Kitching. One day in Greta's corner shop, a woman asked me, "Why is your name different from the rest of your family?"

I replied, "The town hall's made a mistake!" Then I went red.

I was sent to Carlton Street School at an early age, where I learned to read and write. Later, I attended Carlton Street Primary School, all part of the same building at the back of Tumbling Hill. The school was austere and unrelenting with its Victorian architecture. I found no warmth in this place. It had wide stone staircases and huge clocks that ticked away the minutes while watching over wooden desks on the wooden floors and pupils impatient with learning—except for me, that is. I loved learning.

I had a great spirit of curiosity and adventure, and I wanted to explore the world in which I lived. From the age of four, I had read books and comics. In the attic, I used to try to produce films by putting a sheet over a line and holding a comic with a torch behind it, but I couldn't project. All I made was a blurry shadow.

Much of the time, my stepfather was on shifts from early morning until the evening, or on nights. Tired and angry upon his return, he would frighten me with the harsh words he hurled at me. Because he said I was ungrateful, I could no longer try to make films, play, or read in the attic. So I read in the living room, hiding behind my book, praying he would not pick on me. But he nearly always did, knocking the book out of my hands and telling me I'd be sent away to a home if I wasn't grateful.

Our house was poorly furnished—it was my mother's first real home, but not mine. The living room had mottled walls to relieve the whitewashed glare. My mother made curtains for the window. She polished the oven beside the fire with black lead. It shone. Near the fire was my stepfather's armchair. Facing it on the other side of the fire was my mother's smaller chair. I felt angry about this. Around a scrubbed wooden table were four cheap chairs. Opposite the fireplace was a polished sideboard. Two framed photographs stood here, one of Trevor in a suit my mother had made by hand. He had golden ringlets and sad brown eyes. In my photograph, I wore a blue dress and held a toy dog. My hair was also golden blond, but long and straight, and my brown eyes also held sorrow. I used to think my stepfather called me ugly because my hair was straight.

My stepfather sat near the fire after his meal, smoking his pipe or cigarettes. Then he would cough and spit globs of phlegm that hung sizzling on the fire grate before dropping into the ash. I felt sick, for I would have to clean this and light the fire the following morning. I tutted in disgust, and he would get up, eyes blazing, and hit me.

"You ugly fucking bastard with your foghorn of a voice," his usual tirade went, "don't you know I work my fingers to the bone for you! You'd better be grateful!" I knew he lied; he didn't work for me. Our interaction was never easy. People on the street said he was a good man, a worker. They told me to be grateful, that he had taken me in and given me a name. But the only name he had given me was "bastard."

Secretly, I vowed to earn and pay for my own keep; then, maybe, my mother would love me. I knew my stepfather had power because he worked and was a man. He had a penis. Well, I could get a job, too, and I would pray to God to make me a boy. God had gotten it wrong: If I'd been a boy, my mother would love me. So I prayed and got three jobs, but I stayed a girl. One of my jobs was a paper round. I was too young, but the paper man was desperate for help, so he told me to say I was seven if anyone asked. My other two jobs were running errands for the neighbors in the morning before school. My jobs were my secret. I sought no permission. The paper man thought my father had said I could deliver papers.

During the first week of being a paper girl and learning the round, which seemed to cover half the city, I was tortured by the Torpedoes. This gang, made up mainly of young boys, lived in the same street as the paper man. One evening, as I walked home, I was surrounded by a gang of about ten boys. They asked me if I lived on Tumbling Hill and proceeded to give me an Indian burn on both wrists. I was to inform the Yankee Bon Beanos—another gang—that they were coming to fight. These battles were fought by stone-throwing, with dustbin lids used as shields. Windows of houses were frequently broken. Faces were bruised, and a boy once lost an eye. The issues were always the same—power and respect. From this time on, I, too, competed seriously. My arms were strong, and I could throw stones with deadly accuracy, just as I could bowl the best in the street. In Yorkshire, cricket was revered, and my "googlies" in this game were famous. I learned to climb drainpipes onto slate rooftops and shin up lampposts, swinging from the bar just like the boys. In the street there was a grudging respect for me, but all the same I was called a "funny lass."

One day, in the air-raid shelters on the tips,* I played doctors and

---

* waste grounds

nurses with some boys. I decided to be the doctor, and I told the boys to drop their short trousers so I could examine them. Picking up a stick, I hit each one on his willy. How could a willy make a boy better than a girl?

Before the first working week was completed, I had blurted out proudly to my mother that I was earning four shillings and six pence weekly, adding that I would give her three shillings for my keep. I remember how tired she looked as she scrubbed away at sheets in the tub. I wanted to protect her.

That night, my stepfather told me that, as I was earning money, I would have to pay three shillings a week to my mother. I remember how hurt I felt. My mother had spoiled my own bid to be accepted and respected as one of the breadwinners. I decided to steal money from my stepfather, and I wheedled money out of my mother. Gradually the stealing became compulsive. I could not control it. Later, I would steal cigarettes from my stepfather to give to my mother. "Look!" I would say. "He's left these fags!"* She would laugh and smoke them.

I was a moody child, and my mother said I was very willful. It seemed that each evening a bad report was made about me to my stepfather. Then he would hit me and use those angry words: "Ugly bastard!" It took me a lifetime to admit that my mother colluded with both my stepfather and me against each other to make matters worse between us.

Trevor was followed by the birth of Wendy, a little girl who had golden curls and big blue eyes. At the time, Trevor looked like a popular painting of an angel, and everyone said Wendy was bonny. My stepfather adored her, and in a strange way I was happy for him, probably because I thought he would now leave me alone, but it didn't quite work like that. I was seven when Wendy was born, and I was used to looking after Trevor, taking him to the school around the corner from the street, taking him out into the street and teaching him to throw stones.

---

* cigarettes

Outside their houses in Tumbling Hill, the older men often sat in chairs drinking Guinness. Inside their open doors, their wives, like shadows, flitted to and fro doing their many chores. The men had no light in their eyes and seemed to be resigned to their lot. I recoiled from them in alarm; I often dreamed of freedom from poverty, of justice, truth, and beauty as I gazed at the sky. In the slums of my childhood, I dreamed big dreams. On the hill that tumbled from city road to city road, I vowed that I would become a writer and scholar. And I knew that

> *Soft shadows shield from the harsh gleam of day*
> *They are mockers these shadows they just fade away*
> *Boldly exposing the brutal at bay*

In this case, the "soft shadows" were my mother's and stepfather's pretensions to respectability. I was not wanted and I knew it, but I would show them. Slowly I was withdrawing to an inner safe place. Often I wanted to say, "I love you," to my mother, but the words I spoke said, "I hate you." I didn't mean it, but I couldn't utter the loving words in case they were rejected.

I would do the shopping to try and win my mother's love, yet that treacherous part of me found a way to fiddle the change and to lie. For instance, I would say that Bernard in his greengrocer's shop at the bottom of the street had forgotten to give me the change. And always afterward, I felt sick inside.

As I continued at school, I became aware that I was very bright. I was often punished with a cane for being disruptive (which meant I often asked, "Why?") and for seeking attention. Beaten at home, caned at school, and not really accepted on the street, I was lonely. I vowed not to care. I didn't understand why I needed to learn sewing, hemming, and fancy stitching at school. We were being prepared for marriage, but I had no intention of marrying any man, so I acted up in these classes and was sent to the headmistress, Miss Woodhead, who caned me.

I think I was ten years old when the school nurse sent me home with lice and impetigo. She cut off my hair and painted my head purple with gentian violet. My mother refused to cut the curls of Trevor and Wendy, though they also had head lice.

Trevor was artistic and sensitive. Wendy, the good girl, was confident. Both of them just played. I didn't understand how they could be so unaware of the dynamics between my mother, myself, and their father; they, too, were a part of this family. Wendy was full of bounce. She had lots of presents and loving attention. I used to make her laugh by mimicking the comedian Joyce Grenfell. It was strange, really, that when I did things well no one noticed, but at the wrong times the whole world seemed to be watching.

One day, when I came home after delivering papers, Trevor and Wendy were sitting on my mother's knee. I didn't know that my stepfather was in the scullery at the top of the cellar steps, and I went over to sit on my mother's knee too. The next thing I knew, I had landed on the floor. I felt a blow across my face as my stepfather hissed at me, "You ugly bastard! Keep away, she is the mother of *my* children."

Though I was terrified, I said, "She's *my* mother too." But now I knew: This man hated me.

2

BIG DREAMS

Yesterday, 19 June, would have been my mother's birthday. She is dead now. Today I received my first check from the publishers. The manager of the bank in Cowley Road, Oxford, has agreed to let me use their branch of National Westminster in spite of my overdraft. We had a meeting that helped me to organize my finances. This will reduce the financial stress when I start my M.A. in October. It seems incredible that I am able to receive such help. I feel that I'm taking responsibility for the way I spend my money.

Later I had a meeting with Mother Helen of All Saints, Sisters of the Poor, to confirm my date of leaving. On 29 June, with my dogs, I will move to a boat on the river. I requested to have a party as a way to thank the community. Mother Helen suggested a tea party.

I took my dogs out, saw my counselor, and went to the gym. At the pet shop in the covered market, a woman told me in conversation that on her next visit to earth she wanted to be a man. I laughed and said, "Thank God I've got over that one." How strange, *I thought,* that people still imagined it was wonderful to be a man. *A shudder shot through my body as that most powerful of messages from my childhood flooded into my mind. I paid such a high price for an independence that had for so long eluded and frustrated me.*

On the waste ground of Tumbling Hill, there were air-raid shelters and hillocks. From that vantage point, the scene I saw was one of desolation. There were mills and factories wherever I looked, with tall, dominant, smoky chimneys. The only green I saw apart from that in the park, in pictures, or between the flagstones was the grass that grew in tufts on the tips. The sky was filled with smoke. I gazed at it. There was nothing to lift my spirit here except my sense of adventure and imagination. It was here I would think, *One day I will make gleams of gold where foul waters run and broaden the mind of the fool. But there I go dreaming again. Before I can rise I must live and learn and use my knowledge to write.*

As a child, I felt unwelcome at home, so I looked elsewhere and traveled outward seeking adventure. The cinema was a favorite haunt. I loved "cowboy and Indian" films, and I still have a warmth for American Indians today. I identified with the underdogs; they knew, like me, that white men spoke with "forked tongue." On Tumbling Hill, we said that people were "two-faced"—it meant the same thing.

I saw life as an adventure in which I starred as the brave heroine, and no one was going to spoil my adventure. My curiosity and love of words led me to the city library where I spent a great deal of time exploring books. Consumed by a hunger for knowledge of the world beyond Tumbling Hill, I read anything and everything without direction or instruction. I read about doctors, saints, scientists, geography, history, poetry, psychology, and so on, into novels, particularly by women.

On occasion I went to the Alhambra theater and sat right up at the top in the "gods." Just sitting in a red plush seat in the dark was a magical experience. There was a special moment when the lights went out. Then the music started up and the curtains rose. Here, I saw different worlds with people dressed in funny clothes. I remember *The Song of Norway;* the actors sang and danced, the audience applauded. I was spellbound. Certainly I had entered another dimension, but after the show, I had to return to the grimy streets and dark buildings—Bradford in all its roughness, with no magic to uplift me.

The smells of the city attracted me; some shops would swill their fronts with disinfectant; others would use soapy water and, with a stiff-bristled brush, sweep the grime into the gutter. Two large department stores operated in the city. One was Brown Muff's—definitely for the posh people, with large windows that held my gaze. Ladies stood there all day long, dressed as though they were going to the opera or a dance. Brown Muff's had a doorman dressed like a Yeoman of the Guard in one of my books. The stores smelled of the perfume of plenty. Some day, I decided, I would shop at Brown Muff's, but not for ball gowns. The other, Busby's, "The Store with the Friendly Welcome!" was on Manningham Lane. Busby's smelled of everything from cotton and lace material to perfume, from wirelesses to manicures. At Busby's you could find face cream, lipstick, stockings, school clothes, and evening wear. I watched the window dressers create their magic. They, like Brown Muff's, used doll-like ladies.

The chemist's shop, Raw & Hurst, opposite the town hall was packed with potions and pills for pain, smelling a little like Dr. Silman's office—the surgery on Little Horton Lane—but with the additional smell of perfume and soap. At the butcher's in Thornton Road, I smelled blood. The huge red carcasses frightened me. The odor of the fishmonger's reminded me of the dreams I had of the sea and sailing on a ship. The fish were laid out on slabs. I was there often, for my stepfather ate a great deal of fish because of his ulcer.

The toy shop next to the chemist also sold bicycles; the toys smelled new, there were paints, trains, books, cars, puzzles, and pencils. I thought the windows were too full of goods. I wanted to make these windows works of art like the window dressers did at Busby's and Brown Muff's.

I loved looking at the shape of buildings and chimneys. I was really fascinated by the whole erection of civilization and city dwellings. I wondered how people had the ideas to draw and build things with such precision. I also read the newspapers because I delivered them every day. I read about politics in the *Telegraph and Argus,* but I didn't understand too much. I also read the obituaries; they used to make me feel very sad, and I was drawn to that sadness. But my attitudes were, *You won't beat me, I'll show you,* and *I don't care.* This willfulness of spirit, even though it worked against me in some ways, also carried me through.

I wrote to film stars in Hollywood, and I was sent photographs of Maureen O'Hara, Danny Kaye, Bob Hope, Bing Crosby, John Derek, and many other actors and actresses. I just felt certain that one day I would make films in Hollywood, and I told this to everyone in the street. They would laugh and say, "You believe everything you read in books," and it was true that I did, because certainly I couldn't believe anything I heard in the street or at home. My mother used to say, "Tell the truth and shame the devil," then I would hear her lying to my stepfather and hear him lying in return. People in the street told blatant lies.

By the time I was eight, I, too, had become an accomplished liar. I was a game-player, I could manipulate, and I stole. My incredible ideals remained alive, and I wanted to be upright and honorable and dignified—those words were very powerful to me in my childhood. But with these words were those other hurtful phases: "Ugly bastard," "Funny, funny lass," and "No man will ever want you because you are too intelligent. He won't want a brain. He'll want a wife who will do his washing, bear his kids, and cook his meals." This was not what I wanted. The language used in the street where I lived was one of angry words and abuse, a language that did not allow people to grow and develop. As my stepfather used to say, "Spare the rod and spoil the child." We were subdued by that threat, a fear for life, and a punishing God.

Next door to us, a crowd of gypsies moved into the end of the passage opposite the gas lamp, and they had a horse that they took into the house. My mother was furious about this. There must have been sixteen of them—men, women, and children, all with red hair. All the people in the yard hated them. I'm not sure whether they were Irish, Scottish, or English, but they spoke with a strange accent. They didn't stay long. Shortly after they went, it was true that everyone in the neighborhood seemed to get head lice. I don't think it had anything to do with the gypsies, but they got the blame.

One of the things about the slums that I wanted to escape was the smell. Every day I had to take the bucket that was used during the night, carry it across the yard, and empty it; it was always full, and I hated the smell of its stinking contents. I wasn't very squeamish, but I particularly hated emptying anything connected with my stepfather. I always associated the bad drainage in the street with this, and when I ended up in other slums and other gutters, the smell that always rose to my nostrils was the smell of the drains and emptying the bucket in Tumbling Hill Street.

Because my stepfather was ill, I used to go to Dr. Silman's in the evenings for prescriptions. It seemed quite a long way from Tumbling Hill Street to Little Horton Lane. I now know that it wasn't such a long way, but for a child on winter nights, it was a lonely, dark, long walk. One evening, a man sat opposite me at the doctor's with his legs wide open. I kept staring between his legs because that was where my eye level rested, and I saw a swelling in his trousers. I tried not to look. I turned my eyes away and looked at other people in the surgery, but my eyes kept coming back. He looked at me intensely. I kept looking away. I thought the doctor would never call me. Eventually, I went in to see Dr. Silman, and he gave me my stepfather's prescription.

When I left the surgery, the man was waiting, and he said, "Wait outside here for me and I'll walk you home."

It was a cold, icy winter's night, and the northeast wind was blowing. I said, "Yes, I will," then as soon as he went inside, I ran off down Little Horton Lane, my heart bursting, across Chester Street bus station, down Carlton Street into Tumbling Hill Street. I couldn't tell my mother exactly what had happened because I just knew that I had done something bad. I told my mother that a man had asked me to wait for him, and that I had been very frightened so I had run away, and it was very dark. From then on I didn't go to Dr. Silman's at nighttime; I went on Saturday mornings.

This morning, Wednesday, 21 June 1995, the longest day of the year, I was out early with the dogs, and we went to South Park. I looked again at the college spires, which are known famously as the dreaming spires. The dogs played, and they were free and happy. I seem to have found an equilibrium among greenery, tall grass, very leafy trees, and just me and the dogs in the park.

We came back home and I went to the gym, where I am in the process of making amends to my body for the years of self-inflicted damage. One of the fitness instructors said to me that I was wearing really heavy boots, and I looked as if I was about to kick someone's head in.

I replied, "I don't need to kick anybody's head today because I am a spiritual warrior."

He laughed, saying, "I'm a bit of a warrior too, Chris, but what do you mean, spiritual warrior?"

And I said, "What I mean is that today I take care of myself, that I like myself and I wish harm to no one, but I will not allow anyone to harm me. So although my boots are not for kicking anyone, they are symbolic."

He said, "I could put it more simply: I like me, and if you don't like me, that's all right."

I came back from the gym and took the dogs out again, this time to the river. I looked at the boats, sky, and water and thought about the boat I was going to move into shortly. I liked what I saw. On the way back, I saw a man on the ground. I didn't know if he was drunk or stoned, maybe even dead. Then a lollypop man* yelled at me, "Will you go and phone the police? You live in the convent." I was stunned by seeing this young man on the ground, and the lollypop man persisted, "Can you hear what I'm saying to you?" His tone was really harsh.

---

* crossing guard

I said, "Yes," and went in and phoned the police. I too had lain on the pavement like this man, and people had passed me by not knowing whether I was dead, unconscious, or drunk.

My physicality was so difficult for me when I was a child because I felt I had the wrong body. I remember hearing men at the end of the passage saying things like, "Well, I've got another bun in't oven," or, "She's got the rags on today; I couldn't get any of my oats, get my leg over." They were always going on in ways I didn't like, and it seemed to me that women's bodies were there for the men to abuse. This phrase about "she's got her rags on" really upset me. I couldn't bear the smell of "the curse," as it was called in the street, and perhaps that was another reason for my fear of being a woman, because women's bleeding was called "the curse." There was no respect for this natural part of a woman's function, which produced offspring and new life. I found it really difficult to accept that I, too, would one day have the curse. I remember one time when my mother was bleeding—it was during the war and we didn't have sanitary towels, or my mother couldn't afford them—and she cut up old sheets into strips. I saw a bloodied sheet that had been used to cover her bleeding, and I couldn't bear the smell. To me, this smell, like that of the slop bucket, was symbolic of oppression and of the powerlessness I saw in women's lives, which meant even their bodily functions were shameful.

I saw women in the street, some of them with big bellies and black eyes. The skin of their hands was raw and red, their faces tired. They dressed in mill pinnies,* with their hair in curling pins covered by turbans. In bitter winds, while hanging out washing on lines with pegs, they joked as they smoked their Woodbine cigarettes. (My mother didn't smoke Woodbines unless she had to; she smoked Craven A. I think this was because she had been in service as a maid and had mixed with people who could afford cigarettes that cost more. However, when she had no cigarettes, she was glad to smoke anything.)

* aprons

These women seemed to laugh at the men in their lives. Yet they cooked, cleaned, and ironed for them, slept with them, and had babies with them. Why did they love their abusers? Why were the men so angry and tired when they came home? They cursed and ridiculed the women. I didn't know then that this was one way of dealing with life in the slums. I remember one man saying to his mates, "To shut her up, I've stuck another bun in't oven." He already had a large family. I didn't want his way of life for me.

One of the women in the yard said to my mother, "Phyllis, I know he beats me, but it's just his way of showing he cares. He's a good man, really!" What a funny world I lived in!

When the war ended, there were great celebrations in the streets of the city. We had beaten the Germans, I was told. In the city, bands played and marched; soldiers, sailors, and airmen paraded in front of a jubilant Yorkshire crowd. In Tumbling Hill Street, I saw a man on a bicycle with a curious V-shaped ladder over his shoulder. He climbed a few steps up the ladder and lit the gas lamp at the end of our passage. He was cheered as he went down the street repeating this ritual. Every day, morning and evening, for a long time, he came to turn the lamps off and then to light them again later.

Sometimes I would play outside after my evening paper round was done. Fascinated by the soft glow of the gas lamp in the harshness of the street, I would play whip the top, watching the colors of my spinning top in the light as I whipped it.

Although I was a loner, I did play with friends on the street, and other children seemed drawn to me. I was often made the leader in games. Some friends stand out in particular. There was Hazel, who was a tomboy, and I liked her sister, Pat, too, who had a Mona Lisa smile. Everyone thought she was a lady. Her brother, Keith, was interested in keeping fit. Their mother worked in the town hall, which was a good job, and their father was elsewhere.

Hazel's mother used to frighten me when she stood over me and asked, her green eyes boring into mine, "Do you love your father?"

I would go red and say, "No."

Irene was a girl who lived in the same yard as us, and she was the youngest of a noisy, rowdy family of six. Her father was small, wore a flat cap, and had a fag in his mouth all the time. Her mother was raw boned, slim, and full of nervous energy. She worked in a mill.

I had other friends from the Nassau family. Mrs. Nassau had given birth to sixteen children. Her husband was German, so she had a tough time in the slums during the war. Some of her children were considered mentally disabled. Stanley professed a liking to me. I quite liked him, but only as someone to talk to or wander round the streets with. There seemed to be a hint of getting us together, but I knew this was not for me.

My special friend, however, was John. He lodged with a family that lived near me. He was Irish. His father, who drank, appeared at certain times of the year, usually smelling of booze, and hung around the women. John and I sometimes went to the pictures together and played in the derelict houses. We were real pals.

I call these children my friends, but they weren't real friends. They were just people in the street.

Sometimes I would sit under the gas lamp with some of the kids and listen to their talk. No matter how I tried to fit in, I felt different. They said that I was a tomboy with a gruff voice, not pretty or feminine. I wanted to be accepted but knew I had to excel at everything I did to earn this. Being a bastard carried a stigma; it seemed a bad thing to be. Yet I knew that I'd come from the same place as Trevor and Wendy. So the fuss had to be something to do with my father—mine was not only absent and anonymous, but he hadn't married my mother. Because she was married to George Wilkinson, Trevor and Wendy weren't bastards.

My stepfather was a chapelgoer so we went to a Congregational church that also had a Sunday school. This was the first place in my life I had ever been welcomed with warmth. I remember in particular Miss Oates, a woman over ninety, and Mr. Suddard. These two people had what I know now as a glow of goodness. Miss Oates would tell stories with a crackly, elderly voice, but she didn't have the tired eye or faded cheek of women in Tumbling Hill. Her cheek was still like an apple, maybe past its best, but she was really alive. There was a great love in this woman and nobody played her up, probably because she loved us. Mr. Suddard was a kind man. He didn't have the same gift as Miss Oates, but he was one of the few men in my life who spoke to me with warmth and respect, who didn't abuse me sexually, mentally, or spiritually. He treated me like a child and was very loving to me. He didn't touch me, but I felt a warmth from him.

On the wall in the chapel was a great big picture of children in the world: different nations and cultures, boys and girls, big and little, fat and thin, brown, white, red, yellow, all holding hands. This image spoke to me. Miss Oates told us about children from other lands, about how we were all one human family and that we were all on earth to do something that would help the rest of the world. No matter how small it may seem to us, we all had an important mission to live our lives to the fullest.

At home one day, my stepfather was sitting reading the Bible, having been on night duty. I often felt great pity toward him, but then I would despise myself for feeling like that and would steal from him, thinking how badly he treated me. Very occasionally I tried to be friends with him, but it never lasted long. On this particular day, he told me that no man had ever read the Bible from beginning to end and that he wanted to do it. I saw there was some sincerity in this, but I also saw the hatred he carried within him, which got in the way of everything. I knew he was suffering; he looked so lonely and so unhappy. He wanted to talk to me about it, but suddenly I knew that we could never be friends. I just wanted to get away from him, so I made some excuse to go out. No matter how good my days were, no matter what I did, when he entered into my life he soured it.

As for my real father, I didn't know who he was, only who he wasn't. I sometimes imagined he was an Irish lord who wrote poetry, rode horses, told exciting tales, and was great fun. He knew of my dream to be a great writer, a great scholar, the first female to climb Mount Everest. He knew also that I longed to be a Roman Catholic and go to the Latin Mass, for I believed that, in the church, the family was holy. He knew of my longing and hunger for knowledge. He didn't care that my voice was gruff and that I was like a boy; no, my real father loved and understood me. I wanted to do so many things. Certainly I dreamed big dreams for someone who was just a street urchin.

3

PEOPLE DIE, NAMES DON'T

29 June 1995, St. Peter and St. Paul's Day. Two years ago today, I was baptized in the convent chapel by Sister Jean Davina. Sister Frances Dominica was my sponsor. Bishop John Taylor presided over the ceremony. This event meant a great deal to me and still does. A woman baptized me, and that was important.

The move to the boat brought a sense of relief. I was moving on, becoming more independent. The owner of the boat and his friend helped me move all my belongings. That night I was on my own with my dogs on Gleam, moored on the river in Port Meadow.

Today has been a good day for me, the weather is lovely, and it's the fourth day of Wimbledon. I haven't caught up with John Major's election campaign yet, but I had a meal with the sisters and now I'm sitting with Robin Waterfield in his study in the grounds of All Saints recalling my schooldays.

When I was about eleven, my mother went to Carlton Street Primary School to speak to the headmaster. Mr. Housecroft read my school report, which said that despite being intelligent, I was rebellious, which led to disruptive behavior. Mr. Housecroft told my mother that I loved to learn, and as I was interested in most subjects, it would be a good idea to send me to a grammar school.

My mother told my stepfather. I remember standing behind his chair; I was small and my head didn't come over the top of it. I heard my stepfather saying, "We can't afford to send her to grammar school, but if I earned enough a week and we could afford it, I would be willing to send her. I treat her like she's one of my own children. I've never raised a hand to harm a hair of her head."

I said, "That's a lie," from behind the chair because I just couldn't believe he had the nerve to say such words.

Instead of going to grammar school, I was sent to Prince Vale Secondary Modern. It was a mixed school and rough. My main memory is one of being ridiculed. At that time, I wore my hair in plaits and sometimes the boys pulled my ribbons off. When this happened, I didn't giggle or act silly with them, and they disliked me for not playing their game; so when they pulled my ribbons in the future, they did so in a nasty way. They also teased me about the way I spoke and called me "Boy's Voice." It was known in this school that I didn't like the idea of getting married or doing housewifery, although I could perform these tasks well. I tried hard at sewing because it was something to learn and do, not because it was a domestic skill I wanted to acquire. Domestic chores put women in prisons, and I was afraid after seeing the women in Tumbling Hill and what life had done to them.

Shortly before attending Prince Vale, I had to have a photograph taken for my application to the school. Previously when I had looked in mirrors, all I had seen were big brown eyes and beautiful skin—not many people in the slums had such a clear complexion. Now when I saw my photograph, I didn't see the face exactly as I did in the mirror because I was always looking for the ugliness my stepfather constantly pointed out. I just saw someone who looked like a street urchin; my hair was jagged and untidy, and I looked scruffy. I decided to smarten myself up. One place gave me an opportunity to feel good about myself and the way I looked: the Girl Guides program at the Congregational church on Little Horton Lane. I had to ask my stepfather's permission to join, which he gave willingly because he wanted to be seen in this church as a fair man and a good father.

I was in the Blue Tit Patrol, and eventually I became the leader. It didn't take me long because I was eager to learn and brilliant at tracking, so I got lots of badges for tying knots and learning semaphore and Morse code—I just sailed through these things. My mother was quite proud that I had joined the Girl Guides. For a while, books weren't knocked out of my hand because my stepfather wanted to appear to be supporting me, although he never said so.

The acceptance of the Girl Guides gave me a confidence that I had not experienced before. I could be the hero and leader I wanted and aspired to be. I wasn't ridiculed. Miss Grayson was the captain of the Girl Guides, and she was a particularly caring woman. Not only did she encourage us to develop, but she could relate to us and seemed to understand us.

The Girl Guides went camping on the Yorkshire Moors. I could light a fire with two matches and cook anything over an open fire. I remember a funny incident that happened once as we walked over the moors during a camping trip. There were horses around and one particular horse had an erection. I nudged my friend Julie and said, "Look at that horse's dick," and my broad Yorkshire accent carried in this place where the air was clear.

Miss Grayson heard me. She turned around and with a wry smile said, "Christine." Although I laughed, I wasn't ashamed. I've never forgotten the way Miss Grayson said my name that day, because although she let me know that was not the way to behave as a Girl Guide, she didn't imply I was a bad person.

I felt good in the Girl Guides, although I didn't want to be in it forever. I liked the uniform and I liked wearing a badge on my beret.

People looked at me with respect, and this encouraged me to join the St. John's Ambulance Brigade. I did very well, especially since I had done some first aid in the Girl Guides. However, my interest in the Girl Guides and St. John's Ambulance Brigade began to fizzle out as the traumas that followed in my life drained my energies, sapped my confidence, and brought me back down to those familiar feelings of anger and shame.

After a big row between my mother and stepfather over me, my mother went to court and said that I was out of control. The good that was coming from being in the Girl Guides seemed suddenly to count for nothing. She said I was always out on the streets, and when she called me in I wouldn't come, and even though my stepfather beat me, I would still go out again the next day. To top it all, I was stealing from them. There was nothing for me at home.

I had heard my mother and stepfather arguing about my adoption by him and about my needing his name to go to Prince Vale, but for me the damage was already done. Everybody knew I was a bastard. If they didn't know from the name on the ration book, they knew from the loudness of my stepfather's voice when he hurled abuse at me.

At Prince Vale, I also had difficulties because I was encountering boys in the process of becoming men, and I was developing into a woman. I had a great fear of girls and women and identified far more with the boys. This, in itself, made things hard for me. The boys expected me to be feminine. They ridiculed me because of my gruff voice and my boyish appearance, despite my plaits. It was at this time that I first kissed a girl full on the lips and realized I enjoyed it. Just before I was twelve I had my first period. Now I knew I was truly cursed, because I was a bastard and now I was bleeding. I felt dirty.

I went to court with my stepfather and my mother to have my name changed legally to Wilkinson. It was a name I didn't want. When the magistrate asked me my name, I said, "Christine Wilkinson," refusing to add "sir" as my stepfather prompted me. I didn't say another word, but I thought how heavy my burden had been without this name and how unbearable it would be with it now. My stepfather would never let me forget he had given me his name, and there would be a price to pay.

I used to think that my stepfather had died because he had had to give me his name. Just before he became seriously ill, he was often seen sitting and reading his Bible. He presented himself to me as a very fair and decent man, and I knew that really he was all these things, which is why I was confused by the hatred he had for me. I could never make sense of this, and I didn't know how to talk to him about my feelings. Neither did I know how to win his approval. Just before he was taken to the hospital with a ruptured hernia, I washed his body in bed, fed him, and emptied the slop bucket. I did these duties in a special way, as a service to my stepfather because I knew he was dying. I wanted him to see that I was bigger than the battle that went on between us. Even so, my kindness was not acknowledged and I never had the approval I sought so fiercely.

In St. Luke's Hospital, Bradford, just before his death, he offered me a plate of custard, and one of the guilts that I have carried for years is that I was unable to accept it. I just ignored him, even though he was on his deathbed, because I thought he had offered his kindness too late. When we left, I didn't kiss him good-bye; I just couldn't. He said, "Look after your mother," and because I couldn't do anything he told me to do (no matter how ridiculous that sounds), I knew that I wouldn't look after her. Then he died.

I refused to attend the funeral, although some of the neighbors did. I knew I would be expected to cry, but I wasn't sorry that he was dead. I had wished it so many times. All this anger toward my stepfather, even after his death, made me feel I was a bad person again. Wendy and Trevor were too young to take it all in. Who knows what they were thinking? When he was taken out of the house in his coffin, I peeped over to look at him, to make sure he was really dead. I remember thinking that this was the man who had controlled my life, and now he was dead. There was a sense of loss, but it was easier to hang on to all the hatred and abuse. I helped to prepare the reception after the funeral, although we were too poor to put on much of a show, and then I disappeared.

Two months after my stepfather died, my mother went into the hospital with pneumonia. When she came out, she was completely blind. I had once wished my stepfather dead and wished my mother blind. Now he *was* dead and she *was* blind. I believed there was a badness in me, and because of this I relentlessly punished myself. Anything good in my life I destroyed, even though I cried out "No!" as I did so.

After my mother came home from the hospital, she asked me if I would take her to my stepfather's grave. It was in Scholemoor Cemetery, Lidget Green, on the outskirts of Bradford. It was a cold, late December day, the winter of 1951. I had never walked a blind person before, and I dragged my mother along the path. There was ice underfoot. It was the bleakest of days and it was windy. The trees in the cemetery were black, not just because of their bark, but from the soot. Even clean washing hung outside had specks of soot all over it. The bleakness and desolation of the Yorkshire Moors was present in that cemetery. I began to chatter to my mother about the statues all around us because I felt frightened, and I could sense her own fear as I dragged her along impatiently. I did not know how to help her with her fear, and I certainly did not know how to deal with mine. Then suddenly we slipped on the ice and landed flat on our backs. My mother started cursing. I laughed from nervousness and began to describe a beautiful monument of an angel with out-stretched wings standing above us. This angel did not have an insipid face, but fine and kind features. It stood out against the black and bleak cemetery as a tiny piece of hope.

After pulling my mother to her feet, I found my stepfather's newly dug grave. I asked my mother, "How did you pay for this?" She replied, "It's a family grave, and it will hold four people. I've paid for it from the insurance premium I've been paying out of the family allowance."

"But aren't there five members in the family?" I asked.

"Well, you'll be leaving home, Christine," she replied. "You wouldn't want to be buried here, would you?" I just thought, *I didn't imagine all of that—I really wasn't even welcome in the family grave.* My mother had a strange sense of respectability inherited from working in service for the upper classes, and she knew it was an accepted fact that a bastard was never buried with the family. The rejection and betrayal I felt from my own mother hurt me deeply. I don't think there are any words to describe that sense a child feels at being so utterly rejected. She might as well have said, "You aren't wanted where you live, and you're certainly not wanted in the grave."

Trevor was now nine, Wendy was five, and I was thirteen. I decided that if Trevor and I went away to boarding school, Wendy could stay with my mother. She felt safe with Wendy, and I knew they would get support from the Blind Institute and neighbors. Yes, Wendy would learn to handle my mother's blindness, because I couldn't. I couldn't bear it when she walked into doorways and smashed her nose, or banged her head, or bent down and caught herself on the door handle. This clumsiness made me shout at her impatiently. In time, I did learn how to walk with a bind person: I let my mother link her arm with mine and lead me, and I guided her. My mother also learned to read braille and did some braille reading on the radio. She also started going to the Blind Institute. But something had gone out of her life. She had a lethargy about her that showed me she had almost given up the will to live. I knew that if Trevor and I went away, she would have the space she needed to learn to cope with her blindness. After seeing the school doctor about this, Trevor and I were sent to an open-air school in Wharfedale—Linton Camp School near Grassington.

I have only vague memories of my time at Linton Camp. The overwhelming memory is one of uncertainty and grief. I remember joining in sports, swimming, and gardening; there were few academic classes. One of the boys at the school had a huge head and webbed hands. One of the cruel things that my stepfather had said to me was that I had a big head, and when I saw this boy and heard people calling him "Big Head" I couldn't bear it. I think I was the only person in the school that hadn't called him "Big Head," but one day I looked him straight in the eyes and said it to him. I wanted to see whether it hurt him, but it didn't seem to touch him. I didn't see a flicker of pain cross his eyes, and I thought, *Why does it bother me so much?*

Most of my time was spent having crushes on lots of girls at the school. I had crushes on Caroldene, the head girl, and Dorothy, the deputy head girl. My crushes arrived in short bursts and never came to anything. They were an expression of my powerful need to love someone and to have them respond. This need was what drove me on. As a means of satisfying this desperate longing, I developed a crush on one girl at Linton Camp named Rita. In order to get close to her, I made friends with her brother, but it was Rita I really liked. I had many such crushes. I knew that I preferred women, but I also knew for some reason this was considered wrong, so I always used a boy as a cover. Often, when my feelings were returned by another girl, I would run away and get a crush on someone else. I wanted to love but found it hard to trust others or open my heart. I could give it out, but no one could come in.

At Linton Camp, most of the children were disruptive. It was run on a punitive system, and Mr. Sternwhite, the headmaster, wielded the cane heavily. I was often called onto the platform in front of at least 120 pupils and publicly caned. Every time this happened, I would say, "It didn't hurt," and he would call me back to cane me again. For some reason, I could not stop myself; I would try and grit my teeth, but I would always end up saying these words, and he would always call me back.

I felt lonely and out of place at Linton Camp despite Trevor's presence and my mother's visits. Linton Camp was about fifty miles away from Bradford, and my mother took the bus to Skipton where she changed buses for Linton. When she came to see us, I was shamed by her blindness and the way she looked and dressed. She used to bring us a few bananas and sweets. I did try and share them equally, but sometimes I ate more sweets than Trevor. I wanted to cry because we got such a small amount when other people seemed to have so much to give their children. I felt sad for my mother, but at least she came.

A big exercise that was popular all over England at this time was called "I Spy," and one of its tasks was "I spy in the countryside," which was run through newspapers and in magazines. Big Chief I Spy came to visit us and gave out badges and certificates if we made a certain number of observations, such as "I spy cottages with thatched roofs," for which we marked down where we saw the cottage; or "I spy this bird"; or certain hills or stars. I loved I Spy and I did very well. It fed my curiosity, and I loved the open space at Linton Camp and the clean grass and vast, blue sky. Sometimes I walked to Grassington by myself down by the river. I walked through grass higher than my head, and it felt so good to be close to the earth and away from the dereliction of Tumbling Hill. This was a clean place that was not filled with smoke, depression, and violence.

There was one teacher, Jessie, whom I really liked. She taught physical training and had been to a school called Bolling Grammar. She was tall with blond hair and fair skin; a brilliant swimmer and a good athlete, she was also caring. I decided I would go to Bolling, so I asked if I could apply for a scholarship, and I was allowed to take the exam. At thirteen, I sat my scholarship for the second time and passed. Then I applied for a grant and was accepted.

4

NOT FOR SELF, FOR OTHERS

On 5 July 1995 I went to London to speak on the first national radio station for women, called VIVA. *This had deep significance for me. I felt privileged, not in a creepy sense, but because I had been invited to speak on this program. There were many different kinds of women there, and they all seemed powerful and radiant. There was a tremendous sense of celebration. I met Lynne Franks, who was the presenter of the program. I felt so welcomed and delighted to be there, and I recognized that this was the sort of thing that I had wanted to do as a child and a young woman. There was another woman there, Daphne, fifty-five years old, who had decided when she was fifty to lose three stone* in*

___

* one stone equals fourteen pounds

weight, and three years ago she became a triathlete. She is now up to Olympic class, the top class for her particular age group. She runs, cycles, and swims. To celebrate the opening of the radio station, she rode 965 miles in eight days on her bicycle, her route being in the shape of a daisy round the streets that surrounded VIVA. VIVA *was the heart of the daisy, and the streets around were the petals. When I told my story, it wasn't heavy; I felt I was singing. It reminded me of how in Tumbling Hill Street, at Bolling, and later, I had wanted to lead women in their fight for liberation from oppression. I saw at* VIVA *that these women didn't need to be led. They had reclaimed their own power, and that was empowering for me. I was not only included by these women, but respected and affirmed, too. I left* VIVA *and walked back to the Tube* through the London streets where I had once lain flat on my face, and I felt healed.*

In 1952 I left Linton Camp, and my brother, Trevor, stayed. I went back to Tumbling Hill Street. My mother and Wendy had made friends with a Christian family, the Birkinshaws, and they were amazing people. Mr. and Mrs. Birkinshaw, from Lincolnshire, had two daughters, Ruth and Rosie. The whole family befriended my mother, particularly the daughter Rosie, who was a young, tall woman of about twenty-seven, and full of fun. Ruth was fun, too, but quieter. Rosie and Wendy seemed to hit it off. I had never met a family who actually practiced their Christian beliefs. They were very unattractive to look at—I viewed people with a critical eye and was always able to find some fault, no matter how perfect a face or physique. This stemmed from the barrage of insults I received from my stepfather on my own appearance.

The Birkinshaws helped my mother prepare to move from our house on Tumbling Hill Street, which had been condemned. We were given a council house to rent, probably at the suggestion of the Blind Institute. Mr. Birkinshaw brought a handcart because we couldn't afford a van, and we piled up all our possessions. The fog was so thick the evening we moved that we could hardly see any-

---

* London subway; also called the Underground

thing in front of us. But my mother, even in her blindness, knew the way, and she led us from Tumbling Hill Street, up Little Horton Lane and Park Avenue, to 186 Canterbury Avenue. The house was almost at the top of the avenue, just like the one on Tumbling Hill. I couldn't find it because the fog was too thick, but my mother knew by touching the railings. I didn't believe she would be right, but when I put the key in the door, it opened. I lived in this house on Canterbury Avenue for a few years. The first two years coincided with my attendance at Bolling Grammar School.

The first day I went to Bolling I didn't have a uniform, so I wore the green striped dress I had had at Tumbling Hill Street. It was too tight because my body was developing into that of a woman. In the school assembly of five hundred girls dressed in green with red blazers, I stood out in my striped dress. Even though I felt self-conscious, I was able to focus on the mistress who played the piano, Miss Ledger. I could see she was a very strict teacher, but I took an instant liking to her. I felt that she would be straightforward and someone I could respect. Miss Grayson, the headmistress, who wore glasses and had a mustache, welcomed us all to the school. I had disliked her on sight at my interview, and the feeling was mutual. At the first assembly, she welcomed us all to the school. Then we saw the head girl, deputy head girl, and the prefects, and I was extremely impressed with the school. Miss Grayson spoke of the motto, "Not for self, for others." I didn't want the people in Tumbling Hill Street or anywhere else in the slums to be right about different classes of people. Above all, I wanted to believe that people were just people, and where one lived or the way one spoke didn't really matter.

When I finally got my uniform, I traveled out from Canterbury Avenue to school feeling confident and proud. But nothing was ever just right. I didn't have a new gym slip; mine was patched at the back and I felt ashamed. Because I was fourteen, I was put into Form 3A, which was a year behind the form I would have been put in had I gone to Bolling when I was eleven. This meant I was three years behind with the work. There was no preparation to help me catch up. I had done some preparatory reading, but with no instruction. Miss Grayson had told us that high levels of achievement were expected at Bolling, and it was announced again at the assembly that certain former pupils had gone to university and done well. She used Latin words that I didn't understand. I wanted to live up to this expectation and do really well.

The rest of the first year changed my perception of Bolling. I applied myself as well as I knew how, yet everything that I did fell short. I had the wrong accent for a start, an accent that told everyone I came from the slums. I couldn't detect a particular difference in other pupils' accents, but I began to play up to the slum-girl role. I was cocky to cover up my insecurity and hid behind my roughness, although I aspired to be a prefect. I had lots of crushes on different girls, which were cries for friendship rather than desires for a sexual relationship. I wrote notes, stared, and smiled at various girls in the class; I probably embarrassed them. I was never invited to anybody's home, and that hurt. I didn't know what I was doing wrong. (Recently, I received a card from a woman who had been one of my peers at Bolling, saying she had seen me on a television program, and at last I felt I had some acknowledgment from Bolling.)

I did well in English, and Miss Allsop loved the idea of somebody living in such a romantic-sounding place as Tumbling Hill Street. Of course she had never been there, nor did she make the connection between Tumbling Hill and the experiences I had had in my life, but I liked her and she made learning fun. In class we read books by the Brontës, Jane Austen, and others. I still wanted to be a writer and read anything I could lay my hands on, particularly by women writers. I felt an affinity with Emily Brontë, who was strange and wild and roamed the Yorkshire Moors. Her work moved me.

French lessons were ridiculous. The teacher just put a book under my nose and expected me to teach myself. I had no idea how to go about learning French, having never done any first-form lessons, and being thrown into third-form French was too much. It was then that I began to see that they didn't want me to succeed. I certainly wasn't encouraged to do well. The future of other working-class girls depended on this experiment of letting me attend Bolling Grammar School. It wasn't the highest-achieving school in Bradford, but it was the second-highest, and I was never allowed to forget it.

I tried to relate to all the teachers—I needed to know they were interested in me, and I wanted their attention. But most of them seemed to find me difficult, and the math teacher, Miss Slee, found it hard even to look at me and acknowledge my existence. There were very few teachers I felt comfortable with, and the only person I looked to as a role model was Miss Ledger, the music teacher. She was what people would now term an old-fashioned schoolmistress, firm but straight. She demanded that pupils did their best in her class, and she often got results, but more out of fear than inspired teaching. I was one of the few pupils who was not afraid of Miss Ledger and respected her.

At the end of the first year, I hadn't done too well, but I hadn't done too badly either. During that year I played rounders* and hockey for the first time in my life, and I liked hockey even though it was so rough. All these girls who were going to be ladies were so sneaky with their hockey sticks and would whack my ankles when no one was looking. I had been sent to the headmistress several times for answering back in class, for being disruptive and defiant, so I knew when I was being put down. I knew what it felt like to be a scapegoat.

Life at home was easier than life at Bolling. On a deep level, I did not feel I deserved to be at Bolling. In some subtle way, at home, I had unconsciously assumed the role of my stepfather, with all its re-sponsibilities for the family. There had always been a strong bond between my brother, Trevor, and me, though less with Wendy with all her bonny bounciness; I think her feelings toward me and my go-ing to Bolling were mixed.

My periods at this time were very heavy, and I was often gripped by moods I could not handle. One way of dealing with the mood swings and a deep sense of sorrow was to get a crush on someone. These fixations were a way of dumping feelings that I didn't then know how to deal with, which seemed to be connected with my mother and her family. I used to wonder if my Uncle Arnold had in-terfered with my mother, and though I didn't understand these

* a ball game; similar to baseball

thoughts clearly, I knew that they sprang from sex and from the times I had been abused by men in cinemas or in a crowd. Once, when I went to the speedway, a man put his hand up my dress, and I was too frightened to shout out. It was so crowded that I couldn't get his hand away from me, and I had to endure it. The secret and the shame were confusing. Other thoughts were based on experiences I couldn't speak about because I felt I would be blamed and told it was my fault for being a bad girl.

While I was trying to sort out these feelings, I was also aware that if I didn't go to college, I would have to get married and have children. I wanted to have a relationship with a woman, and yes, I wanted it to be beautiful. I did not want to marry and bring up children.

My anxiety was heightened by my mother again taking me to court and saying I was unmanageable. On a weekly basis, I began seeing a probation officer. She wore a man's jacket, like a Yorkshire writer I had read about called Naomi Jacob, who also smoked a pipe. She insisted her jacket was not a man's jacket, but her jacket. These women helped me to feel I wasn't a freak.

However, I still felt there was nowhere I belonged. On the Canterbury estate, many of the women worked in the mills. By Bolling standards, their language would have been called coarse, although at school everyone spoke with a Yorkshire accent. Many of the girls at Bolling were the daughters of prosperous shopkeepers, police officers, and other respected professionals. Although their background was very different from mine, we all followed the current fashions, which at this time included having a DA hairstyle like that of Elvis Presley. Nevertheless, the whole ethos at Bolling was very different from that of the Canterbury estate. At Bolling everyone aspired to become "a lady."

In my second year at Bolling, Miss Ledger was my form mistress. I was in Form 4L, still a form behind. French had at last been taken away from me. Miss Ledger put my name forward for class prefect and I was voted in. I proudly led my form to and from assemblies, took the register, and did it all so well.

Life was very difficult at home. Trevor was now back from Linton Camp, and money was very scarce. The Birkinshaws took my mother to their church, and often we were given food. The church was a Catholic Apostolic church, led by Mr. Busby, a wealthy businessman over eighty years old who owned the department store in Bradford called Busby's. He paid for a gardener to do our garden and visited our mother. He had three sons in their sixties, and after he had married his housekeeper, she gave birth to a son—so there was also Mr. Paul, aged six. I was very interested in Mr. Busby, and I started going to his services in Little Horton Lane, just off Morley Street. Mr. Busby knew that I wanted to go to college, and he realized the setbacks and the difficulties I had at Bolling. He suggested that if I didn't go to college, I could have a job at Busby's department store.

As the year progressed, I had to stand down as prefect because I swore in anger at one of the mistresses in class, but I was fed up with doing the job anyway. Being a prefect was not what I imagined it would be. Although I still loved being at Bolling, I became disillusioned. I was learning that the people in the slums who had talked about class discrimination in simple terms, calling people toffee-nosed and snobs, were right. This wall that I couldn't break through was not of my making; it had been there long before I arrived. I just kept bashing into it, refusing to learn, thinking that I could change the situation, which was an impossible one from the start. I sometimes wandered around the quadrangle looking into the library, since I had a crush on the library teacher, Miss Round. She was a Spanish woman with light brown skin and very attractive brown eyes. But, as with my mother, the sad thing was that nobody seemed to want my affections.

Then I got a crush on Margaret and Brenda. I used to follow them around. I got myself a boyfriend named Gordon, and I used to get him to take me to Margaret's house. Her mother had a shop in Manchester Road, and I would take Gordon around the back and wait to catch a glimpse of Margaret. One day her mother came out and gave me a box of biscuits and asked me never to come again. I refused to be bought off, so there was a complaint put in to the headmistress although I had never touched Margaret.

Bolling came to an end. I was asked to leave, partly because of my sexuality. Although I was sent to the headmistress about Margaret, the incident wasn't spoken about openly. It was also pointed out that my academic achievement and behavior were poor. The school thought it better that I left and went to work. I was asked politely to leave, but it was expulsion: I couldn't return to Bolling even if I wanted to. Another dream came to an end. There I was back at the bottom of the Tumbling Hill of my life.

The end of my education left me in a world where I had no place to turn; I was lost. I was left with a deep sense of futility, because what I had really learned at Bolling was how to play the game. I had played to win and to take part, but again I had ended up a loser, and I was fed up with losing. If I had had a doctor for my father or the lord mayor of Bradford or the chief constable, as some of the girls had, if my family background had been different, my behavior would have been treated in a totally different way. I would have been given help and support. My sexuality would not have been shamed. I felt I had let down not only myself, but also many other people who were possibly like me—those who had aspirations or might come to have aspirations, but who wouldn't be allowed into Bolling Grammar School. This was an intolerable burden.

My stepfather was dead and my grammar school dreams had been dashed—that was to do with the system—but there was another battle I had to fight, and that was with God. I believed that if I made friends with God, everything might come right. The one thing I disliked more than all others about my mother was that she hated the Irish and Catholics. I loved the Irish because I felt that I belonged to Ireland; I felt more Irish than English and longed to know God as a Catholic. I believed I was being punished by God. I also believed that when I was eighteen and a Catholic, I could become a good Christian, because I knew from everything that people said that now I was a bad Christian.

5

"I'LL SHOW THEM"

6 July 1995. The day of the Wimbledon semifinals. Andre Agassi is facing Boris Becker. This morning around seven o'clock, Bella, Bess, Dancer, and I went for our usual walk on Port Meadow, only today was slightly different. Bess found a way into a farmer's field and started chasing a cow and her calf. Dancer joined in while Bella, the baby dog, was frightened. The cow was protective toward the calf. She bellowed and charged. I was too frightened to get the dogs away and kept yelling at the top of my voice in the quiet Oxford air. The farmer appeared, looking concerned.

I said, "I cannot get the dogs; they will not come for me. If you want to give them a whack, I'll understand." This explains the level of my distress: I knew that there was no other way that the dogs would come to heel. So the farmer actually hit Bess, Dancer set off at a great speed, and I caught him. The farmer took hold of Bess and I said, "I understand your anger."

And he said, "Yes, I am angry," and he looked quite relieved that I wasn't afraid to hear him say that. I put all the dogs on the lead, apologized, then walked away.

The good thing about this was that I didn't feel ashamed of myself or that I had done something bad. I was determined the incident wouldn't spoil my day. The sun was shining and the lush green of the meadow was now filled with cows, bulls, and horses; there were swans, ducks, and their young on the river—it was such a peaceful morning, particularly now that I had the dogs back on the lead. I had a day before me and so much to do I didn't know where to begin, such a contrast from other times. The gratitude I feel now is very difficult to express. I can only show it by my actions.

Yesterday, I was very moved when Mother Helen and Sister Frances Dominica spoke to me when I went to see if there was any post for me. They told me that any debt I had incurred at the convent was wiped clean, that there was in fact no debt. I am not often lost for words, but I went very quiet and I nearly cried. In fact, I owed quite a deal of money, and they were generous enough to give me this gift of freedom from the burden of debt so that I could move forward. Mother Helen also added that my growth while I had been in the convent had been tremendous.

I said to her, "Now I am actually living my adolescence, where before I ran from it. I didn't know how to experience it."

This is my connection with that time between the ages of sixteen and twenty-two, when I was like a child of ten trapped in the body of a woman who had given birth to a baby and had been sent to prison for being drunk and disorderly.

When I left Bolling at the age of sixteen, I was to enter into one of the most harrowing periods of my life. It lasted just over six years. No matter how horrific my experiences were later, these particular years were so difficult to travel through because I betrayed myself. I knew what I was doing even as I betrayed myself, but I could not stop. My mother had always said I was extremely willful, and it was as though a wildness had taken charge of me and I ran amok. I ran into a world of heterosexual relationships. I thought that if I became "normal," whatever that meant, I would be acceptable to society. I abused myself and allowed myself to be abused.

Shortly after I left school, it was decided by my mother, Mr. Busby, and the Birkinshaws that I could work in Busby's department store as a shop assistant. I was expected to wear a black skirt, black jacket, white blouse, stockings, and dark shoes. I went to work with yellow bobby socks, blue suede shoes, and my hair cut in a DA style—which was the fashion then—but I did wear a skirt. I was given a pair of stockings by Mr. Busby, and it was suggested that it didn't suit the tone of the department store to go around in yellow bobby socks and blue suede shoes. My mother was given some money to ensure that I bought a pair of sensible shoes, which I did, but I hated conforming. I just wanted to be myself.

At Busby's I sold dress patterns like Simplicity and Vogue. I was very thorough and willing to work. In fact, I was the best assistant in the department, so much so that I didn't have my own book to write down the numbers of my sales. The buyer and the deputy buyer insisted that I put down the sales in their books, because then it looked as if they were doing very well. Another sales assistant nudged me to put down what I sold on her pad, too. So everyone recognized I had the ability to sell. Did they like me for it? No, they did not. They resented it. They didn't understand why this crude woman with a DA haircut could be of such interest to customers. It was very simple: I paid attention to them. I knew what it was like not to be paid attention, and I respected these people who were spending money.

Mr. Busby, "the old man" as they called him, used to buy all the women who worked in the department store a pair of stockings for Christmas (all the men worked in the offices or held managerial positions). But he didn't buy me a pair of stockings; he bought me an alarm clock to make sure that I got to work on time. Because I spoke in a loud, gruff voice, he suggested that I take elocution lessons. I felt as though a prayer had been answered. When I went to my first lesson, I found my teacher had the shrillest voice I have ever heard in any human being, and it was she who was going to teach me how to speak! I decided that I preferred my gruff voice to this woman's shrill tones, and so we met only once. Nevertheless, I was still very fond of Mr. Busby.

There were two women with whom I became friendly at Busby's: Donna and her cousin Christine, with whom I think I fell in love. I was always dashing upstairs to the top floor past the hairdressing department just to catch sight of this very young, attractive woman. Donna said to me one day, "You look at Christine with love in your eyes," and I felt as if I'd let them see too much. I knew it wasn't wise to let people know those things; I had learned that I must stay in hiding.

We had a Lamson system at the store instead of a cash register. This meant that, when ringing up a purchase, we put the money and the receipt into a metal cylinder and twisted it round, then put it in a chute that drew the cylinder up to the office on the top floor, from where the change was sent back down. When customers gave me money, I used to put it in a drawer; I didn't send it through the Lamson. I recorded that we had sold the patterns so that we would get new ones in stock, and with the money I put in the drawer I went out drinking and bought cigarettes, because I had started to smoke. I wasn't very happy about this stealing, but again felt I had no control over it. Whenever I was rejected, I would punish people in a certain way, and I knew that where it hurt the most was in the pocket. Eventually I got caught and was asked to leave. I was told I wasn't a suitable person to be working in a department store. The stealing wasn't mentioned.

While I was still at Bolling, I had started a sexual relationship with a married woman named Barbara, who lived close by our home. This woman had two children, and she gave birth to twins not long after I was expelled from grammar school. She also had two stepchildren, and my sister, Wendy, played with her family. I think our relationship was an open secret. One night, when I had sneaked out to the outside toilet to meet her, her husband came out of the house. It was late, about the time everyone came back from the pub, and I was in my pajamas. He put his hand around my throat to strangle me, so I lied my way out of the situation and said my mother had thrown me out.

My relationship with Barbara was one of great dependency on my part. I was drawn to her even though I didn't find her physically attractive and disliked her personal habits. I began to see her differently than I had during the romance of our early days while I was at Bolling, possibly because of the length of time I had been sneaking out to have sex with her, or possibly because I watched from my bedroom window when her husband was away and saw another man, Charlie, come around. Charlie, a married man with six children, was a friend of Barbara's husband. Barbara and Charlie used to come back from the pub together late at night, and sometimes he went in the house. Other times, they would stay at the end of the path talking for a long time, and often she would look at my bedroom window, knowing I was watching. I had this idea that if I could get Charlie away from Barbara, and her husband away from her, too, then she would want only me. Even though I didn't really want this woman any longer, I had some deep need to know that somebody wanted me to love them. I set a plan in action over the next couple of years to win her, but as with most of my ventures in life, it bounced back right in my face.

Sometimes I would sit and look into the flames dancing in the fireplace in the house on Canterbury Avenue and think of my stepfather and of the dreams I had on Tumbling Hill Street. I despaired, even though I kept telling myself that one day I would go to college, one day I would be a writer—it was always one day. I felt as though I had nowhere to go and nothing to do. I was feeling as though I had thrown away the right to be Chris, and now I would have to get married and have children. I had often heard some of the men say that a good screwing would straighten this woman or that woman out, so I thought that would work for me.

Although I didn't feel it was unnatural to love a woman, Barbara had made me feel shameful by saying I was too easy. She had treated me in a way that I knew was abusive, although I didn't have that word in my vocabulary then. Abusive was just the way a man would treat a woman; she was a married woman and I think that she thought this was how she had to behave. I remember her saying to me, "I can take love or make love."

I became addicted to punishment and abuse. I was extremely promiscuous. In dark cinemas, I let men grope me under their raincoats and put their hands in my knickers. That first feeling of excitement I felt at knowing that somebody wanted to touch me was always followed by sickness and a real sense of shame. It was the same way I felt after my sexual encounters with men and boys in Bradford.

After my job at Busby's, I began working in the cotton mill as a doffer in the spinning room. *Doff* means "to take off," and the work I did involved replacing bobbins that were full and putting empty ones on. There were eighty bobbins to a side, two sides to a frame. Most of the women did piecework (which meant they were paid for the weight of what they produced), so the doffers had to work fast and not confuse the different threads for different machines. It was quite skilled work although it was the lowest position in the mill hierarchy. If for any reason we were slow, we got a great deal of abuse hurled at us. The women working in the mill usually had large families and work to do later at home. They were in no mood to be slowed down.

Because of a number of things going on in my life, I wasn't a quick doffer at the start and took some stick. Then I met Martha, who became the head doffer. She was eighty, with a hump on her back, and she moved like lightning. I copied her movements from bobbin to bobbin, and I, too, became really fast.

The mill was like a prison. It had stone stairs. The overlooker was a man, and if you had too many smokes, you could get sacked at a minute's notice. I worked ten hours a day, and I had three-quarters of an hour for lunch and one-quarter of an hour for a break in the afternoon. It was tough work, but I got on with it.

After work, I came home, or I went to the pub, or I took my mother to the pub. At first I drank half pints of mild, then bitter, then pints of bitter.* I sat with women in a bar of a public house, and

---

* mild and bitter are types of beer

I was bored. I thought, *I can't put myself through this for the rest of my life.* The women all sat in a group getting drunk, and the men passed by on their way to the toilet, or sent drinks over, or flirted with them. I found this behavior so empty, yet I listened because of that part of me that was a writer. I was interested in people, and I knew I was different. I did not like what they had; I did not want what they had. I looked at their faces and saw how hard their lives had been. I could not bear the sense of non-living that hovered around these people.

From the culture of a girls' grammar school, I went to the other extreme, drinking in the city at some of the worst pubs. At first I went drinking with Christine, a friend from Bolling, because I didn't have the courage to go alone. There were some very rough people in these pubs. I would probably call them chronic alcoholics now; then I called them grotesque caricatures of people, and I felt at home with them. This gives an indication of how I felt about myself—not yet seventeen years old, mixing in pubs in the center of the city after two years at a girls' grammar school, and pretending that I knew the score on the streets. Certainly, I learned quickly, although one woman, Beattie, told me that I would never learn. This woman used to take her teeth out when she was drunk, strip off her clothes, and dance on the counter. Some part of me was very attracted to this clowning and revolting behavior of a woman past her forties, who was extremely attractive when she had her teeth in and the drink hadn't gotten such a hold on her. She was also a prostitute. The man she was crazy about used to unzip his fly and wave his penis around the pub.

It was during this time that I became pregnant. Ironically, after all the men I went with, I knew exactly who the father was—Frankie, a soldier. He's dead now. One night Frankie and I went dancing at the Ideal Ballroom, although I didn't know how.

I said to Frankie, "How do you dance?"

And he said, "You listen to the beat of the music and you move to it." I still didn't know how to do it, but I had a go.

Frankie was not a bad man; he was a man of his time and his culture, and he was brought up in a large Irish family in Canterbury.

His family did not like me. When I was pregnant, they wouldn't believe that Frankie was the father of the child, although he said he was and he promised to marry me. I went along with that, and because I was such an adept liar, I convinced Frankie that we would indeed get married.

One night we were walking back from the dance hall and I saw Frankie's brother hit the woman he was with. I said to Frankie, "If you ever lay a hand on me, I'll kill you." A part of me wanted him to do it because I was so angry.

He said to me, "I'd never hit a woman."

But I'd heard it all before. I remembered men saying, "I've never harmed a hair of her head," and yet these same women ended up with black eyes. I never saw Frankie again.

Barbara told Charlie, her husband's friend, that everybody knew I was "hawking my duck"—that's how women talked about other women who were being paid for sex, and at the time I quite liked that saying. Shortly before I gave birth, Charlie invited me out for a drink. We had to walk for miles for this drink because he was a married man with children, and we had sex. I knew we would have to have sex because he'd paid for the drinks, and that was the price he demanded. He felt my stomach and knew I was pregnant, so he didn't want to see me again.

While I was pregnant, I wrote this poem:

> *Now this life within me stirring*
> *Unwanted fruit, man's passion spent*
> *Oh what hopelessness awaits it*
> *What hopes of love and joy ferment?*
>
> *Is there hope for such as this*
> *For with no start how can it end*
> *Will it face this life of harshness*
> *Will it break or will it bend?*
>
> *Oh immortal hands that guide us*
> *Guide this soul in infant shape*

Make the spirit lack the hatred
Ban the mind from all escape.

I gave birth to a son, Michael, in January 1956. I went back to working in the mill after having Michael, and I went out drinking again.
I would leave the baby with my mother, who was still being helped
by the Blind Institute. When I came home from the pub, my mother
would insist that I feed the baby, and when I was too drunk, she
would do it. When my mother could stand it no longer, I stayed
with Michael in a home for several months to give her a break. I resented this baby and didn't know how to love him. I was tired of
women in the street telling me what to do, how to put his nappy* on,
how to hold him, how to burp him—nobody left me alone with my
baby. How could I show any love in front of these prying eyes? I
didn't know what love was, but I did hold him to me quietly when
no one else was around.

One of the things I decided that I could do to be accepted in this
world was to show how much I disliked authority. I fought with the
police and was arrested. I ended up being sent to prison for six
months in September 1956 at age eighteen, for being drunk and disorderly. Michael was placed with foster parents by the social services.
On my first day of imprisonment, I awoke to find myself lying on a
stone slab in a police cell. The none-too-clean blanket did not keep
out the cold, and I was shivering. My head hurt, and I was scared. I
remember being slightly drunk the night before and vaguely recalled
an angry scene with two policemen in the pub at the top of Ivegate.
The eight small panels of glass that let in the grimy daylight fixed my
attention. Over the glass was a grille. I heard footsteps and the jangle
of keys—the noise really echoed around the silent cell. The fear rose
up like bile in my throat as the key turned in the door. A cheerful policeman and a woman called "the matron" looked in at me. They
said something about getting washed. I went with them to a place
where there was a row of cracked old sinks. I washed my hands and

* diaper

face in cold water and carbolic soap and felt a little fresher. I asked about the charge; they said drunk and disorderly and that I'd probably get a fine or a caution. I knew differently but wanted to believe them.

The magistrate said to me before I went downstairs, "You are a menace to society," and as he said it, I felt as if someone had hit me over the head with a very heavy weapon.

Strangeways in Manchester was my first experience of prison. I remember the threatening sound of heavy, clanging doors, loud turnings in the lock, and big, butch women in uniform who terrified me. There were women crazy with anger and frustration. The women's section in Strangeways prison was a very tough place for me. It was grim. It was a very dark building, sooty, smoky, and the humor, too, was dark. It reawakened my defiant inner voice, *You won't beat me.* I was put in the hospital ward where I received night medicine, and I soon learned the system: day medicine for depression, night medicine to make me sleep. I remember there was a woman from Liverpool named Eva, and she used to sing when we got our night medicine. She sang "Red Red Wine." I found it nostalgic. I was missing the pubs in Bradford and the phony air of warmth and friendship that alcohol and certain drugs that I used to buy at the chemist's induced in me.

Once out of the prison, I went straight back to the city center to let them know that I was free. I was quite cocky. I knew that now, since I had been to prison, I would be accepted.

6

WHEN BIRTH BECOMES LOSS

Today, Saturday, 8 July, I went shopping with Isola, who works in the kitchen at All Saints, to choose the drink and the food for my farewell tea party tomorrow on the grounds of All Saints. I was quite excited. It's the first time I've given a party. My mother used to make jellies and custards and was very good at celebrating our birthdays, but this is the first time that I've ever had the courage to throw any kind of a party of my own. In a way, it is a preparation for bigger parties when my book is published and when I get my doctorate. According to the weather forecast, it's going to be wonderful tomorrow. It's the 1995 men's finals at Wimbledon, Boris Becker versus Pete Sampras, and the tea party will take place between three and four o'clock. I hope there will be a television plugged in there in case anybody wants to watch the match. I'd like to watch it at some point as well, but it will be nice also to say cheerio to this particular group of people, who have been exceedingly generous and supportive. Also, it is significant that the majority of the women and the men here are older than I am. I have a great love and respect for older people, as well as a burning desire to halt the aging process, because I do not believe in my heart that people need to grow old and infirm. There are places in the world where people live to great ages, and they don't age in a way that makes them become ill and dependent on others.

Later today, I watched the women's Wimbledon finals between Steffi Graf and Arancha Sanchez Vicario, and Arancha lost. I truly believe that she was the winner because of her spirit and the fight she put into the game. It is true that Steffi Graf is a champion, but I didn't feel that she deserved to win. However, that is often the way the game goes.

When I came out of Strangeways prison, I knew I could never get Michael back. One night I went to the house where his foster parents lived, and I saw that Michael had been left alone in the pram. I had been drinking, and I put my fist through the window, found a way inside, and held my baby to me. Then I got frightened because I'd broken the window, and I ran out without Michael. Walking along the street coming toward me were the foster parents, who had also been drinking. They tried to persuade me to let them adopt Michael. I just couldn't understand why I'd had the baby taken away from me because of my drinking problem, while these people who left him alone and went out drinking were considered worthy of having my child. Nothing seemed to make sense. The world seemed so vast, and I was lost in it, not knowing, at the age of eighteen, how or where to live. Now my battle was with the system, not just an individual. How dared I question the system?

As a way of proving I was fit to keep Michael, I went to Our Lady of the Immaculate Conception in Little Horton Lane in Bradford, and Sister Alicia gave me instruction on a weekly basis. She was my perfect ideal of what a nun should be: She was Irish, her skin and eyes were clear, her teeth were white, her lips perfectly shaped, and she was very beautiful. Did I bestow upon her this appearance? I certainly didn't see this woman with clear eyes. I believed that because of the Hail Mary there was a freedom for women in this religion. I was very confused.

At the same time, I became a resident kitchen assistant at the Park, an institute for the elderly on Rooley Lane. There was a head— Matron Ottoburn, who was a registered nurse—and also a master whom we rarely saw. The nursing staff consisted of sisters, State Registered Nurses (SRNs), State Enrolled Assistant Nurses (SEANs), and auxiliary nurses. There were also other people whose job it was to clean the wards. I worked in the kitchens of one of the big houses. By now I was familiar with the red brick buildings of institutions and the people housed in them.

I didn't like the kitchens too much after the initial novelty of the job wore off. The women wore overalls with white aprons, the cooks wore big hats, and there were big coal fires and ovens used for baking. It could have been in Dickens's time, with scrubbed tabletops, a shiny fireplace that gleamed, and brass to be polished every day. There were also stone floors that had to be really scrubbed. After a while, I'd had enough and had also had a crush on each of the women in the kitchen. Again it was something to do, to fill some longing for a sexual relationship with a woman other than Barbara.

Eventually I went to see Matron Ottoburn. Her husband had some German connection, which was difficult in 1956, not long after the end of the war, and there were often very derogatory statements made about her and her husband. She gave me my chance on the wards as an auxiliary nurse. I took to nursing; it was like a gift. I cared about people, and I was especially curious about how women grew older. I no longer saw the faded eye and wrinkled brow as a sign of beauty; I saw instead the care on these faces, the sorrow, and a sense of bewilderment that seemed to ask, *Is this where it all brought me to?*

The Park had a name that denotes growth, but it was more like a cemetery, as most people who lived there were carried out in coffins. On my particular ward, there were seventy elderly women patients. There were twenty beds down each side of the ward, and down the middle there were fifteen beds on each side of a very narrow partition that you could see through. It was made of a few beams of wood against which the beds rested, so the patients were more or less head to head. In this space there were seventy bodies, seventy human beings breathing out the last days of their lives. I found it very depressing.

One woman I remember in particular. At seven in the morning before I could wash and dress her, I had to put on her artificial leg and her wig. She also had false teeth and wore glasses. I felt she had no joy in her life. It seemed like so much of her wasn't there. I don't know where her spirit was, but bit by bit she was dying. It was strange that I couldn't give my mother this type of care that I could give to strangers.

One night, while I was visiting the convent in Little Horton Lane, a man called for some kind of solace, comfort, and guidance, and he was turned away. I was really shaken up by this rejection. The man was black, and I knew only too well how black people, indeed any kind of foreigner, were treated in Bradford. If their skin was black or if they were Asian, it was a very difficult place for them to live. In some way I felt for this man, and I ran out of the convent after him, saying, "I'm sorry they've turned you away, can I help you?"

He said, "I just wanted someone to talk to. I'm a student." He told me his name was Harry and that he came from Brazil. I went home with him for coffee, and we had sex. I suppose, in a way, that's really all I knew to do; what else would I do with a man? I became pregnant again.

During the months that followed, I left the Park and worked on the buses, clipping tickets. I loved being a clippy, especially when I was on the long return run from Bradford to Harrogate. Sometimes I went back home to my mother, and sometimes I drank in the city. I also worked in the mills. I was sent to a mother and baby home in Liverpool where one of the women, Ethne, was a bully. She'd had her baby and picked on me until I could take it no more, so I grabbed her one day and gave her a good hiding. As a result, I was turned out of the home in Liverpool. I walked down the street and got on a lorry* that gave me a lift to Scotland Road, where I got another lift with a lorry to Bradford, straight back into the guts of the city to drink. It seemed like the pubs in the city of Bradford were the only places I was made welcome.

Then I had to go home to my mother again. I lowered my pride and saw my probation officer, and she got me into the same home I had gone to with Michael when he was a baby. Within a few days I was taken to the hospital to give birth to another baby. I knew that it would be a girl, and I was actually looking forward to giving birth to her. It was going to be different from the first baby. This time I was going to have the little girl I longed for, the baby girl whom I could love the way I had wanted my mother to love me. I was so excited.

I went into the hospital, in labor, and when I gave birth, the nurse told me that I had a little girl. The first words that I uttered were, "Is she very black?" The nurse looked shocked. I hadn't even known that it had bothered me. The nurse said she was very beautiful. When I saw her, I did something that was perhaps very thoughtless: I gave her the same name as me. Christine May Wilkinson was going to be the good Christine, because I was obviously the bad one. When I looked at her it wasn't joy I felt, it was anguish and fear. How could I care for this child? I thought about the prisons, the men, the dishonesty about my sexuality, and the fact that I did not know how to make a home. A little plan came into my mind: I could give her to my mother. *My mother's blind,* I thought, *she sits in a chair, her fingers moving over the braille of her books. She has no interest in her life; each day she becomes more bitter, quiet, and sad. The baby might bring her back to life.*

I stayed with my mother for a while, and there was some drinking, but I wasn't stealing from my mother or anybody else. I was doing prostitution, which I had begun when I first visited the pubs in the city. It was a very strange time in my life. The signs all around me were equally confusing. In the city, instead of trams, there were

* truck

trolley buses now. There was hardly any work that I could not turn my hand to, yet I didn't feel good enough about myself to apply for anything decent. Each job I had worked well until I lost interest. Matron Ottoburn at the Park told me I could still work as an auxiliary nurse, but because of my conviction and term in prison, I could never become an SRN or a SEAN, even though I had a flair for the work. The anger I felt at not being able to become a qualified nurse because of my criminal record was just another bitter pill.

I decided it was time to leave Bradford and go down south to work in hotels. I gave my little girl to my mother. Just before I left Bradford, I had been out drinking, and my sister said to me, "This is the second baby. I hope you're not going to keep on bringing babies home to my mother." She was nearly fourteen at the time, and I smacked her across the face. To this day, I have not been able to say sorry to her, but I've never forgotten it.

I went away with Margaret, a woman I had met at the Park, and we worked in bed and breakfasts in Portsmouth and Southampton. Then we went to Brighton. I wanted to go there because there was a gay scene, although I wasn't sure whether I would have the courage to enter it. Maybe I wasn't really a lesbian after all. Maybe I wasn't good enough to be that, either. Did lesbians go with men? Did lesbians have babies?

As soon as we arrived in Brighton, I went into the pubs with Margaret and met other people on the seafront, and I got into prostitution again. I moved slowly into the gay crowd, sleeping with one or two women, not many, and my whole way of life changed.

Before long, I was arrested for breach of probation on a charge of prostitution and, with a recommendation from the judge for a long period of discipline and reformatory training, I was sent for Borstal training in September 1958. On arrival, I was told that during my stay I would have no social rights other than those the system chose to give me, which were to write and receive one letter a week and to have one visit each month. These were called privileges. I was called either by my surname or my prison number.

During a riot that I initiated, I broke an officer's nose while trying to grab the keys and escape. For this action I was put into a punishment cell with its own tiny exercise yard hemmed in by high walls. For two months while I awaited the magistrate's verdict on my behavior, I spent each day in this barren space on a mattress and sewed mailbags. These were made of thick canvas and had to be made to a specific design. I used a large darning needle and tarred string to sew eight stitches to the inch and remembered being told that "the corners are specially done." This meant, simply, that I had to make a slant instead of a point where the outside bottom ends met. It was hard work.

My breakfast was brought on a metal tray with three compartments, and although I tried to be friendly to the officers, they were formal and frosty. On the tray were porridge, cold eggs on toast, a knife, and a fork. Some time each morning I would be taken out of my cell for a walk around the desolate yard. There would always be two uniformed officers present so I was never able to get a cigarette.

The rest of the day was split into a familiar pattern of meals, work, exercise, and then sleep.

The visiting magistrate finally gave out my punishment for the attack. I lost the three months I had already served and my training was to start again. I was to be allowed back on the wing with the other women but to work in my room sewing mailbags for three months. After twenty-eight days I could enjoy association in the evenings with the others. I was also to lose twenty-eight days' pay.

The system required that I sit by myself in the cell and think about my behavior. In this it was successful for there was little else to think about but my rebellious nature, which would always get the better of me. The discipline and training only served to break my spirit. It added to my sense of failure once I returned to a society in which I felt a complete outcast. Even now, so many years later, I cannot say what I got from it, only what it took from me. While in Borstal, I wrote a little verse to my mother because the baby that I had given to her had been taken away because of her blindness and put into the care of foster parents.

For all the tears and heartache
For all the burning shame

For all the dreams I've broken
Please let me try again.

Oh how I wish I were a child
So we could start anew
For all and everything you've done
I'd be so good to you.

Even though it's bad poetry, it was a recognition of how badly I had treated my mother and an attempt at proving to her how much I cared about her and our relationship.

After leaving Borstal and returning to Bradford, I was raped and I became pregnant for the third time. It happened when I had gone to visit my son, Michael. I came across some Pakistani men I had known when I was at school, who had come over to work on the buses. One of them, Lativ, had liked me, and while the others held Michael, Lativ beckoned me up the stairs. I knew that these men would drop my baby if I didn't follow Lativ, and I knew what going up the stairs meant. The men were throwing Michael up in the air and catching him by his limbs, so I had to do it.

I left Bradford, went to Brighton, and eventually gave birth while staying on E wing in Holloway prison, which was being used as a Borstal Recall wing—the same wing where Ruth Ellis, the last woman to be hanged in England, had died. I had been sent there for a breach of my Borstal license while I had been in Brighton. My son Lawrence was actually delivered in a hospital just outside Holloway prison. A prison officer who had befriended me sat there while I gave birth. I knew that I could not keep this baby because he was born as a consequence of rape. When he was six days old, I signed his adoption paper and he was taken away from me. When he left me, my body was covered in a rash, from my face to my feet. I have never had such a rash, even when I was bitten by rats on the streets. I felt ill. I hated my body.

I felt like an ancient being. I looked at my skin, once beautiful, and it was like the skin of the people who slept waiting for death in the Park. I knew that I had traveled from childhood to old age and

I'd missed out on something. When I looked around me in E wing I didn't like what I saw—ugliness, conflict, enmity between people who were in prison together—and I hated the system more and more. I began to wonder what the word *human* really meant, because I certainly didn't understand it. I became more and more detached from other people and was drawn into a different world, where drugs and prostitution lived. I was drawn to a different kind of music, the music of the nightclubs, the streets, the Beatles. I wasn't too keen on the Rolling Stones. I was more interested in what the music did to me than what it said. This was all part of a drug culture. Prison, too, was part of this lifestyle.

There was some warmth in my life, and this was brought by a prison officer named Elizabeth, the one who had sat with me and held my hand while I gave birth to Lawrence. She was very caring toward me. She was leaving the prison service to go to Australia. My memories of my time on E wing were warmed by the support and friendliness of Elizabeth. Throughout my life there had been people who offered me warmth, but I didn't know how to use it.

When I left prison I returned to Brighton, where I sank deeper into drink and drugs. I was now taking Dexedrine, an amphetamine that was available by prescription to people who registered themselves as addicts. Before going to prison, I got Dexedrine on prescription from a doctor in Brighton. Sometimes I got drynamil, popularly known at the time as purple hearts. I also drank stimulants. The drugs lifted my mind above the fear and confusion, and for a while I was able to think. It was as though I traveled to the end of the universe and back, then when the drugs wore off all the enlightenment I had glimpsed was gone and I was left wondering what had really happened. I was back again in a flat, mediocre, and horrible world in which I felt I was an alien.

The worst six years of my life had come to an end. Six years highlighted by loss. Everything I had, I seemed to lose. Even when I gave it away with good intentions, it was taken away or spoiled. I didn't know then about the sins of the fathers in the way that I understand them today. My awareness of the sins of the fathers today is the shame some feel for being a woman.

After going back to Brighton, I ended up in prison yet again. During this time I went through a reflective period. I knew the sharp edge and the sharp vision I used to carry had somehow become blurred, and I wrote this short poem:

> *This taunting hell of life*
> *This tenacious transit before the hereafter*
> *Gone now the dreams, the illusions*
> *Only a flatness prevails*
> *With a grim continuous existence*
> *And occasional flights to a plane above*
> *Where contentment hides*
> *Elusive contentment*

Most of my life seemed futile. I didn't know where it was going. I was caught in culs-de-sac of nightmares and desperately sought a way out of the sooty blackness that engulfed me. I thought, after the birth of my third child, that this was the lowest I could ever feel. I didn't know at this time that the nightmare had barely begun.

II

"I'LL DO IT TOMORROW"

7

MIRROR IMAGE

This afternoon, 10 July 1995, I sat by the side of the river on Port Meadow, my new home. The dogs played in the river. It was hot. On the other side from where my boat is moored cows and horses were playing and celebrating the water. I had never seen such a picture of joy and fun. One horse lay on its back kicking its legs in the air. For a moment, I ached to be able to paint this glimpse of heaven on earth. I drank the scene in. I saw a man with a ruddy face walking along the riverbank with a pike in his hand, his dog beside him; he was living in a little tent by the riverside. He had long red hair and a long red beard. He was very friendly.

Later, when I walked in the city streets in Oxford, the pavements were hard and hot underfoot, and the sun beat down upon me. I put *my baseball cap on to protect my head. People were hot and stressed and pushed each other to get on their way quickly. I thought what a contrast it was to the peaceful, yet active, scene by the river. I found myself in the familiar cut and thrust of street life, and I began to re-member those first steps toward a life that led me to hard city streets.*

Within the hierarchy of women prisoners, professional criminals were the cream: the shooters of policemen, the shoplifters of dia-monds and gems, and the robbers of banks. Political prisoners were respected, although few of us knew what they were about, and they occupied the status of the elite. Thieves followed next, with burglars further down. I was never quite sure where women who killed fitted in, but they seemed set apart from the rest. Low down on this value scale, I drew a small amount of respect: petty thief, drunk, and pros-titute. In prison I would only take so much crap from the guards and was often put on report. Some of the women thought I was mad. I didn't run with the in-crowd. Despite being afraid of some of the women, I was physically strong and able to fight.

In 1961 I left prison again, and the train rattled on through the Sussex countryside taking me back to Brighton. Before the train set-tled into the town, I felt a pang for the prison I had left. I had been told what to do and how to do it, and I was suddenly left with days stretching before me with no meaning or order.

I stepped down on the platform at Brighton and tasted the salt sea air. The sun shone as I made my way instinctively down to the seafront. The sky was gray and swollen, the streets wet. The pebbled beach stretched drearily from beyond the Palace Pier to the West Pier. I walked by the dark and heaving sea. Most of the cafés and stalls were closed, but the smell of O'Hagan's fish and chips floated on the air.

I had bragged to people in prison of the life I led in Brighton, but on this day I could see its emptiness. It was lunchtime, and the dull day continued gray and flat. Where could I go? I had five pounds that had been given to me by the prison service. That wouldn't last long. I also had a letter for the state money and national assistance that was supposed to help me until I found employment. I knew my way around Brighton, and I knew many people who lived there. However, I didn't want to end up sleeping with men for money, not even matelots* or gay men. I couldn't go through the agony of giving birth again and giving my baby away.

I went to 4 First Avenue, and Margaret, my friend from the Park, opened the door. "Oh, it's you! I didn't know you were out. Come in, I'll make us a cup of tea." As I walked inside she said, "You should have been married years ago," and I just shrugged. Margaret lived in a bedsit† with her baby, Mark, who was almost two. His father was a gentleman farmer who had treated Margaret well, but she said she had spoiled the relationship with her temper and drinking bouts. As I drank my tea, Margaret agreed to let me stay for a few weeks. I felt so relieved. This was at last some sort of home, if only for a while. After egg and chips, Margaret gave me the address of Joan, an ex-lover of Margaret's and of mine, who lived on Montpelier Road. I decided to go and see her and arranged to meet Margaret later in our familiar haunt, the Belvedere Beach Bar.

Big blond Joan greeted me warmly and told me she had missed me. "Each time a sailor left my bed," she said, "I wrote you a letter. I kept them for your return." She gave me all these letters, and we had sex. I knew it would be for the last time.

I made my way to the Belvedere Beach Bar. It was raining. Before going into the bar I walked along by the sea again; it was black, heavy, and rolling. The night, too, was black. Scattered on the beach were fishing boats. It was always difficult walking on this pebbly beach. I loved the seascape at Brighton, which held an austerity that drew me in deeply, giving me the same feeling I got from empty streets and prisons. There was no richness in these places, just isolation and bleakness.

This night the wind started the Belvedere windows rattling, and the rain came in through the doors. As fast as the doors were closed, the wind blew them open again. In front of the mirrors and the bottles of spirits was a woman named Queenie, who ran the bar. She

* sailors
† one-room apartment

was perhaps almost sixty, with glasses, permed hair, and a very precise dress code: she always wore suits with a brooch on the jacket. In her eyes, I saw something that frightened me. I had known Queenie for some time now, and I had never been able to communicate with her.

Other people drifted into the pub: Joan and Margaret; Bunny, a gay boy; Betty, a dyke; and some of the prostitutes who worked the seafront or slept with matelots for money. I bought a round and had a whiskey. I wanted to feel part of the group, but it didn't work. The jukebox played a dreary song by Billy Fury. Everyone kept saying how quiet it was.

Then the wind blew the door open and a woman came in whom I had never seen before. For some reason her presence irritated me. She was tall and slim and wore a long mac,* which hid her body. Her hair, cropped very short over her forehead, was wet through. She strode up to the bar in a way that commanded my attention. She spoke in a well-educated voice that had no Brighton accent, and her movements were those of an upper-class person, a lady. Perhaps that was what irritated me. She had high cheekbones and small features. Everything seemed very delicate about this woman, yet she exuded a tremendous strength. I looked at her in the mirror, and she knew that I was watching her. She wore shades even though it was raining, and occasionally she lifted them and drank. She then told everyone she was going out to see if she could pick up a punter, which was what we called our clients.

My wonderful illusions were instantly dashed. This was a lady who was a prostitute as well, and somehow, even though I had seen this kind of thing in the cinema, it didn't seem to fit. The weariness in her eyes was the clue that gave her away. After she left the pub I felt an absence. I heard later that her name was Jean. Certainly something had happened when she came in, for I could see that she, like me, did not belong. After a few more whiskies, I went back to Margaret's place and slept.

A couple of days later, I got a job in a car wash down a narrow lit-

---

* raincoat

tle street in Brighton, where I worked with three men cleaning cars. Bunny, the gay boy, had helped me get the job, which I didn't really want, but which would use up some of my time and bring in some money. When I wasn't working, I spent hours gazing at the sky and sea and drank in gay bars and clubs. I was popular among the gay men in Brighton, but not so popular among the women. Although I found them attractive, I felt like a freak beside other women; I felt beneath them.

Mr. Smith ran the car wash, and the three men who worked under him were all named Joe. The oldest of the Joes came from Brighton, and the younger two from Malta. One Maltese Joe was big and flash with a handsome face and dazzling smile, and his mate was smaller and slimmer. These men knew Bunny was gay, and they read my sexuality from the way I was dressed. There were nudges and winks and lots of saying "Criss" over and over again. I shrugged off the taunts, and eventually we became friends.

A few days later, while at the car wash, I heard a voice say hello to me, and I recognized a dyke named Julie. We chatted in a friendly manner, but I didn't trust her. By her side walked Jean, the woman I had seen in the Belvedere. Today her hair was purple, and she was dressed in black trousers and top. Julie turned to me and said, "Chris, this is Jean."

She raised her shades with one hand and hinted a wry smile while gently shaking my hand. "How do you do?" she said politely.

To which I replied, "How do you do?" And I wanted to laugh. Suddenly I liked her; I sensed her playfulness.

"See you soon," said Julie, as they walked uphill away from me.

The Maltese Joes laughed as they told me that Julie was a ponce* who sent Jean out to earn money and beat her up if she refused. I told them they were talking rubbish. I remembered Julie working a place called the Jokers Club when she was fourteen or fifteen, where she had sex with men for money. I kept this to myself and let the Joes have their fun.

That night, I went home with a bounce in my step and said just a

* pimp

quick hello to the sea. I felt that some magic had touched me; I felt alive.

The next day Jean came to see me. "I've spoken to Mr. Smith," she said. "I asked him if I could see you for a few minutes, told him I had a message for you." Jean looked tense and tired.

I laughed. "You made me jump. Yeah. I'll meet you in the café across the road in a minute."

"Yes, darling." She smiled as she crossed to the café, moving lightly.

The Joe with the flashy smile winked at me—he didn't miss a trick—and took over my job to cover for me.

In the café, Jean sat with her back to the window. I sat opposite her. She lifted her shades with a practiced elegance and, looking me straight in the eyes, said, "I fancy you gutless."

I gazed back at her, my stomach churning. Her eyes were grayish blue, and as I looked into them I saw myself. I recognized her hunger for life and love. Sensing her agitation, I said, "I'll meet you tonight in the Belvedere if you don't bottle out." Anger came to my rescue.

"We can stay at Betty's; she's an old friend," she replied. "Buy me a tea, darling." And so I did.

As I stood at the counter waiting for the teas, I heard the café door open and turned to see Julie standing there dressed in smart trousers and a casual sweater, her hair greased back. I asked her if she wanted a tea or a coffee, and when she didn't reply, I said, "Fuck you, Julie."

"Sorry, Chris, I'll have a coffee," she said, turning to talk to Jean.

I took my tea outside and left the couple with a cheerful, "See you." I felt strange, but powerful and excited. I knew that no matter how much her angry teenage lover intervened, there was something strong between Jean and me, and we would make love.

Flash Joe grinned knowingly and winked as I picked up my bucket and went to the tap for clean water. "Watch out!" he said. "That Julie will beat you like she does her woman. She doesn't want you taking her wage earner away!" For once, his face showed concern. I assured him I wasn't interested in Jean, but who was I trying to fool?

As I prepared myself at Margaret's place for my date, I thought Jean might not turn up. I washed my hair in the small sink with Vosene and soaked my tense body in the scent of Palmolive. I was worried that she wouldn't want to make love to a body like mine. My stomach bore the signs of childbirth, as did my breasts. If we made love, it would have to be in the dark. I felt ancient again, but when I closed my eyes, I was transported to a paradise where goddesses arrived to make me beautiful. I was surrounded by waterfalls and luscious forests. Two spiritual warriors walked beside me over golden sands, and the moon lit my path with silver.

Outside the Belvedere, I came crashing back to reality. The evening felt cool and damp. The place was full of sailors. Jean arrived, dressed as before in black with her short purple hair cut close to her head. She held her shades in her hand.

"Hello, darling," she sang easily, "I thought I'd never get here. Julie's been tough!"

"Hello, Jean," I replied. "Let's get out of here, shall we?"

Jean took my hand as we walked past the dark sea. Black waves crashed on the pebbles, and the boats lay huddled together.

Harrison's bar was filled with people when we arrived. Two hippie men were playing jazz, one on a clarinet, the other on a sax. The big, butch dyke who played the piano was inviting day-trippers to come up and sing and dance. The atmosphere was friendly and smoky. Whiskies were brought to Jean and me from admirers or punters we both knew and serviced. We raised our glasses in salute and drank. I found it hard to talk to Jean and thought that any minute she would leave me and spend time with someone more interesting.

"I'm supposed to be out earning," she said at last, and I realized then that the Joes at the car wash had spoken the truth. Julie was her pimp.

"Did you tell Julie you were meeting me?" I asked, the whiskey working at last.

She touched my hair lightly and laughed.

"I'll be beaten up if I don't take any money back, darling. Of course not."

Suddenly I felt strong. "She won't beat you. If she does, I'll have her."

Jean looked at me teasingly. "We can spend the night at Betty's, and I'll bet you a pound I get a beating."

I grinned. "You're on. If she beats you I'll pay you the pound and beat her as well." I believed it, for this woman made me feel powerful.

We left hand in hand, and as we were going down the ramp toward the Belvedere, Jean said, "I wish you'd known me before I was past my best. I was considered very beautiful when I danced for Madame Rambert's company. I was much younger then. I'm much older than you." She sounded so wistful.

"Jean," I said, "you are still beautiful. You move like a leopard, and when you speak, my body burns. I've never met anyone like you." My words sounded clumsy to my ears, but I meant what I said with all my heart.

We met Betty, and on the way to her place we stopped off in Preston Street for coffee. I went down an alleyway for a pee, and on my return a cab pulled up. Julie looked out and asked me if I had seen Jean. She told me that she was concerned that Jean may have left Brighton for London to go back on heroin, and that for the moment Jean was on a temporary "cure."

I looked her straight in the eyes and lied. "No, I don't know where she is." Luckily, she believed me and left in the cab. In the café, Betty gave Jean and me a couple of purple hearts. Jean swallowed hers without a drink. I told Jean I had seen Julie and had found out that she was a heroin addict.

Jean and I slept together at Betty's place on a mattress on the floor. We made love hungrily; our bodies danced together. At last, this was the beautiful experience I had yearned for, no longer the crude groping and quick tricks of my recent past. Jean kissed the scars on my arms, the results of self-inflicted wounds while I was in Borstal. She thanked me for our night of pleasure. From her I learned about jazz and ballet; she had opened up a new world to me.

No breathtaking sunset could ever replace this experience for its beauty. I didn't tell her how new all this was to me, nor that I'd never experienced such delights.

When I arrived back at Margaret's place the next day, she asked me if I had stayed with Jean and told me that everyone knew I had. She warned me that Julie would be after me. I told her that Julie didn't bother me, and I made my way to work at the car wash. It was another dull, gray day. The magic of the night before seemed to be vanishing. Again I was alone and lonely. As the drynamil wore off along with the whiskey, I cursed the sea and kicked at the pebbles.

At work I felt moody and ignored the Joes. I caught sight of Bunny and asked him for some pills because I couldn't get to the doctor's until the evening. He had just collected his prescription and offered me some Dexedrine. I bought ten for a pound, took them to the café, and swallowed four with a drink. They would help me get through the rest of the day. Jean and Julie strode past the car wash, and I watched them through the café window. Jean felt my gaze and glanced at me, then quickly away. She lifted her shades briefly; her left eye looked bruised.

The next night, I saw Jean with Julie in Preston Street, and Julie told me I owed her a pound. I confronted Julie, and she smacked me in the mouth. Then I smacked her back, and the two of us were rolling around in the road, fighting, with Julie on top of me.

Eventually I said to her, "This is daft, this is so stupid. Whether you beat me or I beat you, it's Jean's decision who she wants. We could do this all night and get nowhere."

So Julie got up and we all decided to go to Betty's and sort things out. I wasn't sure whether I wanted Jean as my partner, but I went along. Julie sat near Jean and wrapped herself around her. There was no discussion; we all waited for Jean to decide. I got tired of waiting and was about to leave when Jean spoke.

"Wait a minute, I'm coming with you," and she came.

For the next fifteen years, we were seldom apart, unless I was in prison or a drug unit, or Jean herself was in the hospital. If we weren't in some institution, we were together, and it was usually on the streets.

8

CARRIED BY THE TIDE

12 July 1995. Today is the famous Twelfth, and the Orangemen are marching in Belfast. I saw them on television this morning, and I hope the peace holds in spite of all the tension the last few days. I went to the convent to clear out my books and my papers from the flat that I have vacated. It is a difficult experience—a moving on, a changing—and I am very aware of the conflicting emotions surrounding all changes. The point is that these days, I am very aware of my emotions and what is going on within me and around me, whereas before, I sought oblivion and escape.

Jean and I found a room in Regency Square looking out over the sea in Brighton. I had to learn to live with Jean's terrible cravings for heroin. Sometimes this craving took on a presence of its own, as if three of us lived in the flat, not two. When Jean was in the middle of a craving, she became more vulnerable, childlike, manipulative, and needy. In 1961 England, there weren't any cures for heroin addiction, just methods to get people to stop for short periods.

Our room in Regency Street was filled with jazz, cravings, and passion. I remember buying a Billie Holiday record and listening to Dizzy Gillespie, Sarah Vaughan, Peggy Lee, and many other jazz and soul singers. Sometimes the music eased Jean, and sometimes it didn't. The only way I could help Jean with her cravings was to get drugs for her. I would go out to score some Dexedrine or pick up her prescription for it from the doctor, thinking at least she wasn't taking heroin.

I was also taking Dexedrine, and for the first time in my life, I took the coat off my back and sold it for drugs. It was an oatmeal-colored knitted jacket, with leather panels at the front, and it had been the best one I owned. It didn't get me much Dexedrine, just enough to get through the next few hours. It was a significant beginning to another way of life: From now on, nothing was as important as drugs.

As I became more involved in the drug culture in Brighton, Jean and I moved away from the pubs and parties and became more isolated. I walked by the sea and felt strange, as though I were being drawn into a place I had never been before, a place of deadness, and yet it was almost seductive because it seemed full of excitement. But it was really about getting away from what was going on in our lives—about getting stoned. Sometimes I would see the world around me so clearly, then the Dexedrine would wear off and I would be blank. I would take more Dexedrine, and I would hear music in a way I hadn't heard it before; when it wore off I was more deadened than before. I felt that the way I was now moving was freeing me from certain expectations of a society that had hemmed me in, and that with Jean and the drugs I had found my home.

Jean became pregnant by one of her punters, and an old friend of Jean's, named Grace, helped us out. Grace was married with children of her own, and she took care of another woman who was a prostitute with children. Jean told me (and I don't know if this was true) that Grace had worked for Jean's mother as a maid. Grace was certainly very fond of Jean, and they seemed to share a special bond. Grace also sold drugs and had access to Dexedrine and drynamil. I helped Jean give birth to a baby girl in a room in Grace's house. Just before she gave birth, she asked if she could have a couple of Dexedrine, and she was given them. Kelly was born, and she looked like a miniature Jean. Four days later, Jean and I left Brighton, and Kelly stayed with Grace. Grace was manipulative, and so Jean agreed to give her baby to this woman who was not the wisest of parents but nevertheless would love this child because she had always wanted a daughter just like Jean.

Jean and I went to Southampton and Portsmouth. Jean worked in a brothel in Southampton, and I cleaned cars. We stayed in a bed and breakfast. The landlady opened the doors of her store cupboard in our presence, and my eyes were drawn to the biggest bottle of Dexedrine I had ever seen. We took the drug all night and left with the rest in the morning.

Freedom never lasted long. Before long, we were both picked up; I was arrested for failing to report on probation, and Jean was taken to Brighton to be charged for nonpayment of a fine. Jean and I ended up on B wing in Holloway prison.

Holloway was one of the few places in the world where I was greeted warmly, usually after having been told harshly by an officer to strip off and put on a dressing gown. We were given the prison uniform of green dress, green cardigan, gray socks, and black shoes, all of which had been worn before by someone else doing their sentence. We then had a bath while one of the prisoners who worked in reception brought up a cup of tea. They were always friendly because they wanted to see what we had come in with, maybe some smokes, drugs, or money.

B wing always reminded me of a ship. It had a broad bottom and cells on either side—the B1s. The basement was covered by an extremely heavy wire safety net sufficient to hold the weight of several people. In the early morning and evening, just before we were locked in, alcoholics who were constantly in prison could be seen scurrying around under this wire with their buckets, fetching water or emptying their slops. Upstairs were the B2s. A long railing went all the way around the rectangular wing. This level had a wooden floor apart from where the wire stretched over the basement. Two-thirds of the way along the side were iron steps arriving at iron landings. At one end of B wing, there was a window that went from floor to ceiling; the other end was boarded up from the center.

B wing was a place for people with sentences ranging from a few days to two years. A three-year sentence could be served partly here and then transferred to F wing. B wing was always a busy place because people came and went and came again, and I was one of the familiar faces. I was given a cell with a bed with a very thin mattress, soap, a wooden washstand with a bowl on it and a metal bucket under it, and a chamber pot with a lid. In one corner, there was a triangular shelf, a wooden table and chair, and a mat on the floor—that was it. In the spy hole there was usually a piece of round glass, the size perhaps of a ten-pence piece, but most of the time this glass had been broken by the end of a broom so that we could get cigarettes and roll-ups, which we made ourselves, in and out.

Jean arrived on B wing, and she was frightened. She had never been in prison before. She was given four months; I was serving six. She was off heroin at that time but was smoking dope and drinking. I told Jean that I wanted to work in the kitchen. She begged me not to because I would have to be away twelve hours of the day, and she wanted me to be with her, but I wouldn't listen. Jean smoked heavily, and in the kitchen I had access to dog ends,* so with a little wheeling and dealing, I ensured that she had a smoke last thing at night. Jean was assigned to the paint crew and soon made friends with the women there. I was worried because there were so many lesbians in this group, and I knew what Jean was like. My suspicions were proved right. Jean started hanging around with Esha, a woman I knew from Exeter prison. I watched them getting closer. I tried to put it out of mind and tell myself that crushes happened in prison, but something went cold inside

* cigarette butts

me. Esha was another addict, although I wasn't to know this until a much later date.

Jean eventually finished her sentence. The night before Jean left, Esha tried to stab an officer with a fork, and I pulled her off. I wanted to give her a good hiding myself, because I knew that this drama was because of Jean's release, real Borstal-girl behavior. Esha was locked in. The next morning I said cheerio to Jean and heard her going to Esha's cell to say good-bye.

Jean was a Roman Catholic, and the plan was that she would stay in a convent in London's Chelsea district until I came out of prison. I was very upset and disturbed after Jean had gone, so I went to see Esha just before she was moved from B wing and put on report for attacking the officer.

Sister Young from the prison surgery, on whom I had had a crush, gave me a pile of letters from Jean to Esha and locked me in a cell and told me to read them. Esha, who also liked Sister Young, had given her the letters for safekeeping because she knew that after the stabbing, her cell would be searched. When I read their love letters, something died inside me, as it did when my mother brought my stepfather into the home when I was a baby. I wouldn't speak to Esha for over two years because of her relationship with Jean, apart from saying, "Hi, any gear?"* if I suspected she had drugs, or, "Are the fuzz around?"

Six weeks later, I left Holloway prison. I gave the letters back to Sister Young that day. Jean turned up to meet me. I didn't know that she was going to be there on my release because she hadn't written. We went to see a Paul Newman film in Chelsea. After the film ended, I got us a room just off Cheyne Walk without thinking about what I was doing. We settled in and worked as cleaners at the Royal College of Surgeons until some money went missing, stolen by a dyke named Kenny, and we lost our jobs.

This was my first experience of London, and I soon got to know the clubs and where and how to get drugs. Jean went back to hustling and disappeared for long periods. Sometimes we would meet in

* drugs

nightclubs in the West End. I would put pennies into a one-armed bandit* trying to win money, and I'd watch people dance, not wanting to get caught up with lots of bodies. I was taking a lot of drynamil and Dexedrine, and Jean was always absent, which troubled me.

A few months later, Jean met me in a club in Wardour Mews and said, "I have to go to a doctor and get registered. I've been taking heroin, Chris."

I'd seen her cravings, but I hadn't seen her gouching out† before. Her voice was toneless. I felt terrified to the pit of my stomach. I agreed to go to Dr. Naftalin on Gray's Inn Road.

The doctor asked me, "Do you think Jean should go back on heroin?"

I had great respect for this man at the time, and I looked him in the eye and said, "If you cared about her state of mind, I think you would give her a prescription for heroin."

"What do you know about her state of mind?" he said.

I replied, "I've lived with her for over three years."

When Jean was registered on heroin, our whole way of life changed. Every time she had a fix, she entered a dark tunnel, a place where I could not go. I would say, "Jean, Jean, come on, get with it." I didn't understand. Eventually we lost our room in Chelsea. We spent nights in nightclubs and short periods in public toilets. Jean suffered from kidney trouble and her legs swelled up. I found a basement in Harrington Square and got money from stealing or selling Dexedrine. I couldn't be bothered to register, because when I took Dexedrine, I was always finding things that had been dumped or shop windows that had been kicked in, so I would get a radio or a watch and sell it. Whenever Jean needed anything, I could get it from nothing. It was like magic.

I was fascinated by the people who used injectable drugs. After the first couple of nights that Jean was on heroin in Harrington Square, I started to go and pick up her prescription at Boots in Piccadilly. I met the people from Jean's stories: the African prince; the

---

* slot machine
† having taken too much heroin

beautiful Chinese man; Mandy with her Pekinese, playing at being a lady and not quite making it; and Chris and Moira, two teenagers, almost children, who after having their fix became old people. Although I could sense the incredible pathos and pain these people collectively suffered, I found them attractive. I knew they wanted to be loved, and I felt that I could love them.

One night, when I had taken a great deal of Dexedrine, Jean and I went to King's Cross and met an old lover of Jean's named Gwen. She was on crutches, and her voice was like that of an alley cat in pain. She wore glasses, she picked her face, her skin was dirty and uncared for, and she wore two or three coats. She leered at me, and I felt as though she was waiting to get me. I found out that she had been a nurse and that she had stolen drugs from her patients. She had taken the barbiturate content out of capsules and used it herself. I believe that she had once nursed Jean and fallen in love with her; they'd had a relationship, but now she hated Jean.

Days later I met her again on her own. She was a mess. She stank, and I wanted to vomit when she was near me. But what did I do? I invited her home to sleep on the spare bed in the room that I had rented. She was to be with us for nine months. When Gwen came into my life, something very disturbing came in with her, and I didn't understand how she could gloat over her disgusting state. She knew she was an offense, and this was her power. I would eventually come to a similar state myself.

Gwen never took her coats off, and she always sat up. She took cocaine and heroin, and when she took cocaine, she picked her skin and squeezed the scabs. Her very breath contaminated the air around her. Yet I didn't have the courage to throw her out, because nobody liked her, everybody hated and feared her, and I found myself playing the great martyr. Jean was unconscious most of the day on heroin—every time she had a fix she would gouch out. I would race around the streets, getting money to cook a meal, out of my head on speed. Every second night I went to Boots in Piccadilly to fetch the prescriptions—now I collected Gwen's also.

I was prone to heavy and painful periods, and one time when I had been without sleep for ten days, I came home pouring with blood and crying. Jean was unconscious on the bed. My heart really hurt, and I fell to the floor.

Gwen came over to me and said, "Do you want a couple of jacks, duckie? That will help you feel better." I was terrified of having any heroin and certainly of her dirty syringe in my body.

I cried out, "Jean! Jean! Jean! She's going to give me an injection." Remarkably, Jean sprang out of bed and knocked Gwen across the room. Jean put me to bed and I began to unwind, but I could hear myself going on and on at Jean. I told Gwen, "I can't take it any more, Gwen, you've got to go."

That night I was back to picking up scripts* in Piccadilly. Gwen came to Boots and asked me, "Will you take this half a grain to Jean? I owe it to her." I thought this was strange, but I took the heroin and by the time I had reached the end of Wardour Street, I was picked up by the police and charged with illegal possession of heroin. I was given nine months.

When I arrived on the hospital wing, I was in a psychosis induced by amphetamines. One of the Irish sisters who always made me laugh brought me milk, but in the glass I saw Gwen's scabby face and I couldn't drink it. She changed the milk three times but I couldn't drink it.

I said, "I just can't get this woman's face out of my mind."

The sister said, "I don't suppose that's so strange—she's downstairs on the wing with her crutches." I thought, *I can't get away from Gwen, she's even here in prison.* Then the sister said to me, "Look, she's been here for two days, Chris, and she's still out of her head. She's on paraldehyde, but she's on something else too."

I said, "What do you mean, something else?"

"She's stoned on cocaine or heroin. I'm a nursing sister. I know. But where is she getting it from? Where could she hide it on her body?"

"I don't even want to think of her body," I said.

It was months before I found out that she kept her stash in her crutches. Gwen was certainly a shrewd survivor.

---

* prescriptions

I served six of the nine months in prison and wrote a poem to
Jean.

> *Jeanie where are you now, are you dead?*
> *Killed by the words I left unsaid*
> *Where are you now, where have you gone?*
> *Oh Jean this hurt goes on and on.*
> *Jeanie where are you now and are you well?*
> *No letter comes, can no one tell?*
> *Can no one ease this inner hurt*
> *This inner sob that will not cease*
> *Can no one bring a little ease, a little ease*
> *And me I lay here so alone*
> *Like some repulsive gutted gnome*
> *Where are you now and will we meet*
> *On some dark night, on some dark street*
> *Or will some junkie come and speak*
> *With toneless words that leave me weak*
> *Junkie Jean man's left the scene*
> *She's flying high where torments freeze*
> *A fallen leaf caught by the breeze*
> *But tell me man where have you been?*

I sent the poem to Jean's new address, which I had received via the
street grapevine. Despite everything, Jean was a survivor; she didn't
need me to take care of her. But the letter came back, and I learned
that Jean had jumped out of a six-story window. She had landed on
her feet—the feet of a dancer—and survived, and now she, too, was
on crutches. She had tried to kill herself and had only managed to
cripple herself.

From B wing I was sent by a psychiatrist to St. Bernard's Hospital in Middlesex. I tried to run away, but I ran into the arms of a sister. I was put on to a schizophrenic ward. I wrote these lines while I
was there:

> *Oblivion, utter oblivion*
> *A veil is lifted*

and flung into the very face of being
Oblivion, paradise inverted.

The schizophrenic ward was very difficult: strange and extremely frightening. I had no control over anything I did, apart from going to the toilet, and even then I had to ask permission. There was a grotesque woman, bloated to about twenty stone by drugs, who was in charge of an enormous bath plug that hung around her waist. Luckily, she liked me, so I managed to get baths.

We sat in rows on the schizophrenic ward facing each other, as if we were going to converse, but we sat silent in our drugged stupor. The woman who sat next to me for the length of time I was there was small and stocky with a strong accent, and every time she looked at me, I laughed. She told me the most tragic stories and I laughed. I said that I wasn't laughing at her, it was just the way she told the stories. And she would say to me, "Oh, it's all right, dear, I know you're not well. I know it's your nerves." I had had Largactil before, heavy doses of it, but I had never equated laughing with this drug.

There were thirty women in this ward and no curtains around our beds. Some of the women were extremely aggressive although they were under medication; some had horrific dreams and screamed in the middle of the night. What I remember the most was waking up in the morning and for half an hour feeling happy, refreshed from sleeping, drug free. I would wash and have some breakfast, then I had to get my drugs and the day would be more or less over. I just sat on this chair with the others and laughed.

When I was in the hospital I saw a film called *The Opium Trail*. It was about heroin addicts, men in prison in Singapore, and how they were weaned off drugs and became fit and healthy. But the minute they were released, they went back on the streets. Although it horrified me, it also excited me, and I made a decision that I would take heroin and be with Jean. After my release in 1966, I became a registered addict for heroin and methedrine.

9

PICCADILLY, SUBWAY 4

13 July 1995. Today, walking across the convent grounds to Robin's house, I experienced a great wave of sadness. This is partly because I am leaving the convent and clearing up my final belongings, papers, and books, but also a much deeper sadness lurks. Much of the sadness is centered around the area of Piccadilly, and in particular Subway 4 and the women's toilets. It is impossible for me to tell a story that is straightforward about the years spent on the streets of the West End of London. I can only give some imagery, pictures, some undetailed happenings, chaotic meanderings, seemingly going nowhere—the experience of one addict on the street and these recollections today.

Jean left the hospital with both legs in plaster, and she walked with sticks.* I had to find us a place to stay, so I went to the Simon Community. There I met a man called Anton, who ran a community in Kentish Town called St. Joseph's House, and he said that Jean and I were certainly welcome to stay. Jean arrived by ambulance and we settled in, sharing a room with four other women and sleeping on trestle beds.

At nighttimes, I was back at Boots to pick up Jean's script. One night I met Elsie, a Scottish woman I had known in prison, who was also an addict. I asked her to give me a fix, and she refused. I told her if she didn't, I would get one from someone else, so she agreed to share half a grain and some methedrine. She put some heroin in a syringe and injected me. The experience felt as though I was riding a bicycle effortlessly in the sky. It felt wonderful.

Back at the Simon Community, I could hear myself talking in that junkie voice, and Margaret, a probation officer from Cardiff who was very fond of me, hit the roof. While she was talking to me, I kept vomiting, because my body was not used to this new drug.

Within nine months Jean was walking again. They had said she wouldn't walk within two years, and that this was incredible.

I was by now crazed by methedrine and began selling drugs on the street. Although I used heroin, I was a speed freak and always off my head. I used to go over to Piccadilly during the day, and I spent a great deal of time just standing there while my mind raced. I watched people pass, people going somewhere, and sometimes I used to shout: "Where are you going? What do you do? Are you happy? Who are you behind your clothes and briefcase? You are all strangers to each other, but you are all going in the same direction." I felt I was a cut above these people—I knew I was intelligent. I felt apart from the winos, junkies, hustlers, and gangsters, too. When I looked into the wild eyes of a speed freak, I couldn't see myself, and I just thought they couldn't handle their drugs. I longed to travel, but I compromised, thinking, *Piccadilly is a famous place; the world will come to Piccadilly, and I will see the world that way.*

---

* crutches

My experience of riding the bicycle in the sky was never repeated, although I chased it and chased it, which meant more fixes, more fixes, more fixes. I was friendly. I took people to clinics and helped really sick women out of the toilets, women who had been out hustling so they could buy drugs from me or other people. I really believed I was doing something good. Now that I was registered I felt I was something—a real addict.

Piccadilly looked different. Eros was still there, and Boots was on the south side of the Underground,* a few seconds' walk from the exit from the ladies' toilets. There were telephone booths upstairs in the Underground and cameras controlled by the inevitable station police. In the course of any day, hundreds of addicts would come through. There would be lots of music and noise, and there were cafés with cream cakes and teas. There was Lyons' Corner House, where addicts used to congregate and eat sweet cakes, because when they were junk sick they needed sugar to give them energy. I spent endless futile hours in Lyons' and in the Dilly.† Life wasn't going anywhere; it was always the next fix I was chasing.

After an addict got his or her script, he or she would sometimes confide in another addict the name of a doctor, or agree to give the name of a doctor in return for half a prescription. Doctors widely exploited this practice. In 1968, the drug clinics opened and there was an increase in addicts. People got prescriptions and they worked the system. As a registered addict, if you were searched by the police, you could cover yourself. You could also claim unemployment benefit or sickness benefit if you could be bothered to go and sign on. It was also possible to sell your script. Lots of men came to Piccadilly with bottles of drugs to sell at a reasonable price. If you sold a couple of ampoules, say, for a fiver,‡ you could buy a bottle of barbiturates and make maybe thirty quid§ by selling them again. Then you could buy some speed, or you could run for somebody, which meant finding customers who wanted the drugs. You either got a fix for this

---

* London subway; also called the Tube
† Piccadilly
‡ five-pound note
§ one quid equals one pound sterling

or you got money. Sometimes you got nothing, so you took your chances.

Jean and I moved around but always found somewhere to sleep, whether it was a bed and breakfast, a hostel, a squat, the back of a lorry, or somebody else's house. I made sure she always had somewhere to rest because she suffered from arthritis and angina and was a very sick woman.

If we went to Hall's the Chemist to pick up our scripts, we would go down to Piccadilly toilets and have a fix of heroin or biseptone. In the seventies, I moved on to biseptone linctus, but Jean would give me a couple of her heroin pills and I would give her a couple of amps of biseptone, and we would mix the two. Then I would go looking for some speed and sell a couple of amps, then buy some cigarettes for Jean and tobacco for me. I was a very heavy smoker. There were always people looking to score, either on their way to work or coming from a club. If they'd just slept on the streets, some might even try to borrow a fix. Depending on whether I had any cash or enough drugs for what I needed, I might give them or loan them a fix. Although I was known as a greedy addict, which is a funny thing to say about any addict, I wasn't mean. That was to come later.

Then I would get some Ritalin or sulfate and go back to the toilet, where Jean would be reading a book. Jean read every day of her life, if she was well enough or able to. She might be painting her nails or putting on some makeup. Her appearance was very important to her. We would have another fix, and then I'd be off, off and running, and before I knew it the day would be done. I might remember to get us something to eat; we might even sit in a café and talk some kind of talk, in our drugged states. Once, in a café, I borrowed the price of a cup of tea for Jean and me. Then I stole a big, thick chocolate cake. Usually the manageress had some respect for me because I always paid for what I took, but this day I was really stoned and there was blood left on my hands after I'd injected myself. I put the cake under my coat, and she stopped me and made me give it back. I was amazed to see that, despite the blood on my hands, she put the chocolate cake back in the case to sell again. Then she barred me and only let me back in at a later date.

About this time, Jean and I had a room in Kentish Town, on Malden Road not far from the Simon Community. Downstairs there was a one-eyed Canadian, Jerry, who lived with Daina. Daina's twin brother was a friend of mine. Daina was not my friend. One particular night I was too drug sick to accompany Jean to the chemist—I was beginning to get really bad withdrawal. I don't know how Jean coped with hers; I think she did superbly. I felt as though my legs had gone; my stomach hurt, as did my back, and my every breath was an effort. One moment I would sweat, and then I was cold. Jean said she would go and sell a couple of hits and get a cab back. We were now picking up at midnight at Bliss's Chemist on Willesden Lane in Kilburn. Addicts constantly changed their chemist because of the hassle they got from other addicts waiting outside to score from them or to rip them off, so they kept ducking and diving.

Jean returned from Bliss's and came upstairs. I hadn't had a fix; I was still very sick. Somebody called me. When I went to the door of the room, Jerry was there with a broken bottle in his hand, and he and Daina pushed me and jammed me into a baby's pram at the top of the landing. I was terrified. I knew this man would put the bottle in my eye. He would do it for nothing and would certainly do it twice as quick for some heroin. They came into our room, took our drugs, and went back downstairs. Jean was left unconscious.

Eventually I got her to come around. She was angry and went downstairs to borrow half a grain from Jerry, promising a grain back the next time she collected her prescription. He knew that she would do this, because if she said she'd give double, she gave double back. When I went down, he wouldn't let me have any heroin, and I begged him to let me borrow. He said, "You can have a couple of amps and a couple of Rit," and so that's what I had.

In the morning I had to pay him back. Daina came to the chemist with me. I had to give Jerry three amps and pay for the Ritalin, which I picked up on a prescription from a private doctor separate from the drug clinic. I gave Jerry a handful of Ritalin for the two

Ritalin he had let me have. Ritalin was priceless at this particular time, but a deal was a deal.

I always kept a syringe down my socks, up my sleeve, or in the lining of my coat or jacket, and in a matchbox I carried my needles. This was the equipment I needed at all times in case I got a fix. I injected people in the ladies' toilets in Piccadilly: I would put on a tourniquet to pop up their vein, and I got them a hit straight into the vein, drew the blood and pressed the plunger. Some people spent hours messing around trying to stab themselves with needles, but I had a very clinical and clean attitude.

Jackie, a Canadian, drank Coke, and once she gave me a sip in the toilets. I nearly choked because it was about ninety parts rum, and the can was just a cover. She was also a registered heroin addict. She was not a pretty woman according to convention; nevertheless, she did her best. She spent hours putting on her makeup in front of the two-way mirror, behind which the toilet attendants sat. Most of the time was spent putting on black mascara. Another addict named Frankie would put on false eyelashes and then mascara them. Frankie and Jackie became obsessed with achieving the perfect eyelashes. Frankie often left the toilet with half a dozen eyelashes glued to her cheek. After I had been to the chemist one day to pick up my script, I had a fix in the toilets, where Jackie was applying mascara, staring with stoned eyes into the mirror. I left to hit a doctor for some Ritalin and some tuilin, and on my return to the toilets five hours later, Jackie was still staring in the mirror stroking her eyelashes with a black mascara brush.

There were ten ladies' toilets in Subway 4 of Piccadilly, and most days, at least eight of these were filled with addicts in some state of intoxication, either completely stoned, attempting to get a hit, or withdrawing from drugs. Addicts came here to plan some kind of scam, have a quick time with a man to earn the money to go out and score their drugs, or to count or hide their drugs. I even saw one person practicing forged signatures so she could go out and do some checks. We changed our clothes and washed ourselves in the toilets. We washed our hands and faces in the washroom, and sometimes we washed the bottom half of our bodies with water from the toilets. All this activity meant that there were only ever two or maybe three cubicles available to the public. The toilets were often packed with people who were not drug users, and they must have witnessed some horrific sights. At this time, I did not like the toilet attendants because they exploited us. Often they threatened to get the police unless we saw them right with fifty pence or a couple of quid. The toilets were a world within a world; people had sex, gave birth, and died there.

Purges by the police were a regular occurrence. There were many police forces in and around Piccadilly: the Underground police came and searched us, then passed us on to the Vine Street police, who would swoop down with their vans and drag us out. I was usually handcuffed because I would not lie face down and have some man put his foot on my head. I could have gone quietly, but instead I struggled against this treatment for many years. There were also SPGs, of the Special Patrol Group, and these were usually plainclothes officers who carried guns when there was a big raid. The head of the SPGs was a very genuine man who wanted to stamp out drug addiction because he had two daughters whom he hoped would grow up in a drug-free society.

Ambulance people came in on a regular basis with stretchers and carried out women with needles in their groins or in their arms, which had to be removed. Sometimes these unconscious bodies did not return, and sometimes they came back furious that they had been taken away in an ambulance. Many died. This is where my great sadness and pity lies, for the many women who died or became travesties of human beings in the Piccadilly toilets, while I am still miraculously alive. I saw these women go to prison or onto drug units and come back looking healthy, on so-called cures. Before long, they would return to the toilets, and within a week or ten days they looked like somebody out of a concentration camp.

In the late sixties and early seventies, there was an upsurge of hippie talk about peace and love. With my cynical eye, I just laughed at all these people speaking beautiful words and then going in the toilets and sticking needles in their veins. Peace and love, but war to me. War on my body, abuse to myself. Where was the peace? Where was the love? People said, "Oh Chris, you're a really beautiful person." Sometimes it was good to hear words like that, but I knew they were as superficial as the people.

There were so many characters in Piccadilly, people like me, people from the street that I knew like a dislocated family. I remember One Leg Tommy very clearly. He was a Scottish guy who had an artificial leg that sometimes he brought with him to Piccadilly and that sometimes he lost. Tommy was a very gifted artist. He used to draw chalk pictures on the pavement of the Underground. If you were trying to score a fix off this man while he was drawing, you would be there for hours. I always believed that this was a controlling game he played to make people wait because he was holding the gear. We weren't particularly good friends, Tommy and I, perhaps because being a game player myself, I saw through him.

Esha, the woman from Holloway prison who had had a relationship with Jean, was always around. We swapped pleasantries, or at most, questions about where to get gear or when the police were planning a raid. Everybody seemed to admire Esha, and I couldn't understand why. I once asked her, "Why do so many people like you and nobody likes me, Esha?"

"Oh, it's your karma," she said.

"So what is it with you?"

"I'm just cunning," she replied, and it was true.

I didn't like anyone spoiling my hit. I remember one time when Janet, a woman with a deep gin voice, had just got a hit in her groin, and as I got mine she screamed my name. I yelled at her, "Janet, you fucking ruined my hit." Jean gave me another jack of heroin and I took more Ritalin, but each time I got the hit she called out my name again. The third time this happened I was very angry. I climbed over the toilet wall and there she was, unconscious with the needle in her groin. I took the needle from her groin, opened the door, and got an ambulance. Before the ambulance arrived, Janet was awake and refused to go with them; she still wanted a fix.

There was a hierarchy among junkies—those who had put in a certain length of time using and were still alive earned a great respect, especially from up-and-coming junkies like myself. Canadian

Danny had used for years, and everyone looked up to him. Jean herself had used for nearly twenty years. Habits were given names—a New York habit, an Ontario habit, a Quebec habit—all these places were linked to addicts, because people would go on a so-called cure, only to move and start their habit in a new place. A New York habit was a pretty bad habit because it was rough to survive there. London attracted addicts from all over the world, many of whom were talented artists and musicians.

Belfast Ronnie, who I think is dead now, was a man I dearly loved. He was slightly taller and stockier than me, and we could have been brother and sister. The police would sometimes call me Ronnie and sometimes call him Chris. He was one of the gentlest and kindest men I met on the streets. He was very intelligent and articulate. He was also known as one of the most violent, although he never hit women. He slept in the tunnels under Piccadilly, and we often met. One time somebody came down to Piccadilly selling barbiturates. At that time, sentences for heroin were so high that people couldn't take the risk, so many of us, although we still took heroin, more often used barbiturates, including Ronnie. One person who hated addicts, as many people did, sold Ronnie poisoned barbiturates. He was admitted to the hospital and became like a child. I went to see him in Tooting Bec Drug Unit. He wore a nappy and could only just speak. Another addict, Sonya, suffered severe brain damage. The police approached me, because they knew I was a barbiturate freak, and told me they thought somebody was trying to kill people who took barbs, and that their motive was revenge. Did I know anybody who had been down that particular day, and had anything happened to me? For some reason, this person hadn't approached me. I was scared, because I was known to sell barbiturates, and I feared that I would get the blame.

One day I saw the African prince, Jeff, on the street. He was all dressed in white. He said to me, "Chris, watch yourself, you're walking in dangerous paths." I found out a week later from Jean that he had died of an overdose a few days before I saw him. It was not a hallucination.

The streets, nightclubs, and toilets of the city, although heavily tinged with sadness, also challenged me, and I found that in spite of all the conflicting things I saw, I held with me a great love of the music of street life. I heard the street vendors selling their fruits and vegetables, and I heard others trying to get money out of people with the dice and the cards. People sold leatherwork, woodwork, postcards, paintings—anything it was possible to sell was sold around this area, and I loved all this activity. I traveled through the music of the streets. From the jazz I had grown to love, to the music of the sixties, seventies, and early eighties, the sounds gradually drifted into the background like the hum of the traffic. Everything blunted. The smells that I had once loathed no longer bothered me. The hordes of people were an energy that no longer attracted me; I feared them. They represented the chaos of my own life.

10

BEATEN

15 July 1995. Yesterday morning, as I walked the dogs on Port Meadow, I noticed the weather turning toward autumn. The refreshing breeze was a relief after the past few hot and tiring days. I haven't completed my departure from the flat in the convent, and it seems to be dragging on, but I hope this weekend will see the end of it. I am still having a problem letting go of my intimate connection with the convent and moving out into the world. It reminds me of my desire to leave Piccadilly and to stop taking drugs, but then finding myself saying, "I'll just have another fix and think about it."

All through the night it rained, and I was kept awake. The rain was so heavy I felt frightened. This morning, on my way to the convent to work on telling the story with Robin, I passed through the wet streets of Oxford, which were packed with people. I was quite amazed at this small town so crowded, and I thought of the troubles in the former Yugoslavia, the ethnic cleansing, and the utter disregard for human life. I wondered if this explosion of people everywhere is in some way engendering this. There are so many of us, who's going to miss a few million? Killing is going on all over the world. What purpose are we serving? So many hordes of people are going into shops to buy goods, wandering along the streets— is this part of some plan that, as a human being, I don't know about? Again, I am taken back to Piccadilly, where I used to watch people passing by and ask where they were going. What were they doing? What was the world all about?

The years went on with the same endless round of getting a fix to get out of it, getting another fix to get out of it, and so on, from dawn to dusk or dusk to dawn. Drugs controlled our lives. I started stealing Jean's heroin, and I couldn't stop myself. One night in the telephone boxes on Willesden Lane, she saw me put an extra pill into my fix and she mentioned it. I said, "Oh, no, it was a pill that split down the middle into two, there's only two in there really, there's not a half a grain." She just looked at me and knew I was lying.

Jean's health was deteriorating rapidly. I remember watching her put a needle into an abscess to burst it because the pain was driving her insane. I watched the filth come out of it, and the stink made me heave. She was regularly hospitalized for her arthritis, her kidney trouble, her angina, her abscesses, and for cardiac arrest. By now Jean was very emaciated, and her beautiful body, of which she had been so proud, was a mass of bones. Even so, I still saw her as beautiful, even when she had all her teeth taken out. Somehow there was a magic about this woman. I remember Jean standing in Piccadilly one winter wearing a tatty, old fur coat and no shoes. She stood there posing and pouting. Jean had a lovely shaped head, and her hair at this time was bleached. Men came up and kissed her feet, and I couldn't believe it. She was a wreck and at the same time beautiful. I didn't know how to stop her wasting away.

There was nothing malicious about Jean, who was a devout Catholic. It was as if she were playing at being grown up. But then there were periods when she became what I have experienced in my- self: an old crone. She seemed to know everything that was going to happen in my life. Those times she would tell me about her love for her young sister Patsy, who had gone to join a contemplative order in a convent. She told me that Patsy had had thick red hair that reached down to her bottom, but on her entering the convent, it had been cut off and sold. Jean never tired of telling me this story. Jean also spoke of her other sister, Anne, who was a doctor of phi- losophy. She was proud of Anne, but adored Patsy. She spoke, too, of her two children, Peter and Paul, and her two husbands, one an American. When she was in this state, she would tell me stories of her past, then she would cry and tell me about her mother, but more about her father, whom she loved. He was an alcoholic.

I met Patsy when Jean had to go to her Aunt Meg's house in Croydon for the first time in fourteen years, after a spell in the hos- pital for kidney trouble and yet another abscess. Aunt Meg was close to death herself, and Patsy had left the convent to come home to care for her—she was allowed to break her vow of silence while at home. I went to Croydon every day after selling some drugs to give Jean spending money to buy cigarettes, so she would not need to ask Patsy or bother her aunt.

One day I arrived at the house, and Patsy was sitting at the desk by herself. I sensed the hostility between us. I knew Patsy was jeal- ous of me. Patsy had been Jean's baby, and now she wanted to look after Jean herself. "Do you ration Jean's money out?" she asked. "Do you need to bring her money to her every day?"

"Yes, I do," I replied. I couldn't tell her sister that I had to go out and sell drugs to get the money to Jean.

Patsy laughed and said, "I'll take Jean off your hands when Aunt Meg dies."

"I don't think you need to do that," I said. "It's quite possible Jean could die before your Aunt Meg does. Look, Patsy, you're not the saint in this family. It's quite possible that Jean is." She gave me the strangest of looks. I called out for Jean and Patsy told me that she would be back later and I could wait. I said, "Jean will never en- ter this house again. Jean has left this house."

"How do you know?"

"I don't feel her presence here anymore," I replied. I never spoke to or met Patsy again. When I left the house, I found Jean in Piccadilly.

Jean came closer and closer to death. I, too, was quickly deteriorating physically. My determination to score drugs when I was sick, for Jean and me or for other people, quickly ebbed. Addicts would come up to me and say, "Is anybody coming with any gear, Chris?" as though I knew.

I would reply, "Oh yeah! Someone's coming," and I would be there hours later, waiting, and in the end they always came. It was sometimes the little man from the East End, Jewish Sammy with his trilby hat, his suit, his glasses, and his cigar, with the bottles of barbs that he sold, talking out the side of his mouth. He always wanted to sell by the bottle. If I didn't have enough money, he waited while I ran around and got a few customers. What I actually did was get the money off people, go and buy the bottle, let them have a few barbs, and make some for myself. I knew it was like playing Russian roulette every time I put a needle in my vein. I knew that I could kill myself, particularly when I used sulfate, because I didn't know what it was mixed with. I wanted so much to stop using, and I couldn't. I was afraid to.

Jean and I never planned where we would meet or when, because it never worked; we would be stoned and turn up hours later. But we always found each other. Even when we had had a row, or I had slept in someone's bed or a doorway and Jean had slept elsewhere, we always met. It was uncanny.

One day Jean was sitting on the toilet with the door wide open, as addicts did, and Esha was talking to her. Esha and I had buried the hatchet after I had said how stupid it was not to get on when we saw each other all the time, scored drugs, and even overdosed together. This particular day we'd just had a fix when Gwen walked in.

Gwen looked at Jean and said, "You look like a hag!"

Esha replied, "You've got some room to talk." For a moment I saw Jean through Gwen's eyes, and when she had gone, Jean cried.

"Darling, do I look like a hag?" she asked.

I said, "I think she just said it to shock you," and I could see Jean didn't have the energy to beautify herself.

At around the same time, we were pulled into the office where the Underground police and the Metropolitan police worked. A nasty sergeant named Sue had all the women from the toilets rounded up. She herded about thirty of us in a small room and made us strip off. Jean's bra was padded with dirty tissues, and Sue made a big fuss about looking through all these tissues for drugs. Even the other addicts looked away in disgust at what she was doing. Jean was so well-spoken that everybody recognized this behavior as a way of humiliating her.

My barbiturate taking had become uncontrollable. I was in and out of Tooting Bec Drug Unit and was taken to the hospital for overdosing. I would arrive home, wherever home was, at all hours and in varying states of distress. This must have worn Jean down. I told Jean I was going to stop; I meant it but couldn't do it. Jean seemed more into heroin than any other drug. Although I was ill, too, I focused on taking care of Jean. I took her to places known in the street language as "spikes"—women's hostels in which you were bathed, checked for lice, and put to bed. Jean hated this treatment, but she was filthy, as I was, and she had to endure it.

One day I had access to a large quantity of sulfate. Jean and I took loads of it and then went to a clinic on Hampstead Road because Jean was feeling ill. Sister Sharp, a German, was very fond of Jean and was concerned about her condition. I promised Jean I would get her a fix, and I gave her a small amount of sulfate. We left the clinic and went to Euston station toilets where I gave Jean another fix of sulfate. I thought she was going to die as she got the hit. I gave myself a hit and then, seeing how ill Jean was, took her back to the clinic.

Jean was admitted to University College Hospital, then transferred to St. Pancras Hospital. Her condition was related to her kidney trouble. When I went to visit her that first evening, I was told by the sister not to give her drugs or sneak any inside. I had the remainder of Jean's heroin in my pocket. Because I was an active addict, I took it. I felt guilty about this action because Jean never came out of the hospital.

Over the next two weeks, while Jean was in the hospital, I overdosed twice daily. I took various friends with me to visit Jean. One day the doctor told me that Jean wouldn't last the night. I was allowed to sit downstairs and was told I would be called if anything serious happened. Nothing did.

The next time I went to visit, I brought with me a lovely, gentle man called John, who now teaches yoga, and *The Shoes of the Fisherman,* Morris West's novel of the papacy, which Jean had asked for. When Jean saw me all barbed up, she was extremely distressed and started to vomit. I kept trying to find out why, and this only made her worse.

The sister asked Jean, "Do you want your visitor to leave?"

Jean looked at me and said, "I want you to leave."

The security men were brought up, and I was forcibly removed. I remember Jean tried to speak to me, but all her words were mixed up, almost as if she were speaking backward, and her voice was slurred. She looked so very ill. I knew she was dying, but I wouldn't admit it.

Visiting Jean was difficult, and I just didn't know what to do. I tried to go, I did my best to go, and when I wasn't under the influence of barbiturates I told her how sorry I was. I wasn't able to behave in a loving way. I was so frightened of losing Jean.

I was in and out of Middlesex Hospital, either having my stomach pumped or being slung in a room with a blanket thrown over me. In the morning I would be awakened at 5:30, and I would have a quick wash. Walking down the street, I would see men queuing up* for jobs, many of them alcoholics with the shakes, trying to earn some money to feed their habit. I felt lost. I never knew my way from the Middlesex to Piccadilly, and I was in a constant junk-sick state.

On the morning of 31 July 1976, I knew that Jean was dead.

---

* lining up

I went down to Piccadilly and spoke to a policeman to pass the time—I spoke to anybody to get through the hours. I watched a black man cover himself in a blanket and beg to get five-pound notes. I did some begging myself but only got some coins. When I asked the man how he did so well, he said he scratched himself and people felt sorry for him.

Eventually I phoned St. Pancras Hospital and was told that Jean had died. She had left a message that said, "Tell Christine I love her." I put down the phone and rang again. This time another nurse spoke and gave me the same message. Throughout the day I rang and rang and rang. A part of my mind could not accept her death, and I kept ringing in case they had made a mistake.

I stopped phoning and eventually wandered around Piccadilly. The black man was still begging under his dirty, stinking blanket, which covered his almost naked body. At first he and I were alone, then other people came, and I told them in a shocked voice, "Jean's dead." No one seemed surprised. I told the shopkeepers around the Dilly who knew me, the paper men, the hustlers on the front, the men and women. Then I told the addicts as they came down.

Lady Barbara said to me, "Don't call her back, Chris, she's at peace now."

Then I saw Esha. I went over to her at the bottom of Subway 4 and said, "Have you heard that Jean's dead?" And that was the first time I cried.

Esha said, "Chris, she really loved you. I want you to know that. She really loved you."

"What the fucking hell do you know about what she felt for me?" I said and just walked on.

I met a little woman named Pod, who took barbiturates, and in her very dramatic and well-spoken voice, she said, "Oh well, darling, she's out of it now. You've got to take care of yourself," and I saw that Jean's death was just news to most people.

What was I doing in Piccadilly now that Jean wasn't here? I met Mary, a Scottish woman, and told her about Jean, and she was very sympathetic. People said she was doing it for my prescription, but I really didn't care why. Mary stayed with me for the rest of the day, and the following day we had sex on the toilet floor in Piccadilly Subway 4, after I had picked up my prescription. There were eyes everywhere looking down on us in judgment.

After Jean's death, I went into a traumatic state. Something happened to me that I had seen happen to other addicts, like Jean. They went along scoring drugs and getting stoned, then they lost it and needed to be taken care of. I wanted to die, but I could not. Each morning I came to, went to the chemist for my scripts, and took more and more drugs. The more I took, the sicker I became. My appetite for drugs was insatiable. I was almost always unconscious, flat on my face, flat on my back, down on the pavement, always being propped up and picked up and not caring. Occasionally I caught the glance of passersby walking furtively past me, and I angrily yelled at them: "Why are you frightened of me? Why do you look at me so slyly? Why don't you look me in the eye? What is it about me that you fear? Well, I want you to know that I fear you too."

I became increasingly paranoid, to the point of horror. I was attracted to the repulsive, the dirty, the unwashed, the maimed. It wasn't in a state of grace that I was drawn to such people, it was in a state of need. I sat on the pavement of Jermyn Street and ate bread or rolls that had been dumped in the gutter. I found food, and things to sell, on the street. I picked up dog ends and rolled them in cigarette paper. It seemed that I belonged in the mess, in the rubbish.

There were times, especially at night, when there was a brief, peaceful lull in the craziness of the city. I would stagger around the West End and look at the rubbish bags stacked up waiting to be collected the next morning, at the dirty streets, at the night sky just as dawn was about to break, and I would gaze into the heart of the city lights. The lights did not hurt my eyes; all my senses were deadened. I might turn around and see that someone had had their hand on my arm without my realizing it. Deep inside my very self, I felt so afraid at the loss of Jean. I could only articulate my guilt.

I was sectioned in a drug unit for a year for my own protection. This happened after I found myself dancing down Shaftesbury Avenue and round Piccadilly, finally sitting underneath Eros dressed only in my jeans and a clean white bra. Where had I gotten it from?

A crowd of people had egged me on until I came to and wondered why I was behaving like this.

During my year in Tooting Bec Drug Unit, I became angrier and angrier. I played table tennis, fought with the staff, and was given injections to quiet me down. I saw a probation officer who tried to help me get rid of my grief. How could she?

During the years I was out of the drug unit, between 1977 and 1979, I sank lower and lower, spending most of my time unconscious from overdoses. I slept in doorways in the West End. I was raped one night by a man in Wardour Mews when I had staggered round there looking for drugs. This man had no legs from the knee down. He walked with his hands in a fist and moved on a cart with wheels, like a skateboard. He had the most cruel eyes. I was fascinated by his cruelty and the pain in his face. He had a crazy friend who was stoned and kept putting a knife to his own mouth. The man with the cruel eyes called me to him, and I went over meekly. I walked down the alley and into a phone box with him while his friend stood outside. He raped me, and I did nothing to stop him, nor did his friend. I don't know whether he thought I was a boy or if he didn't care, but he made me bend over, ripped my trousers, and penetrated my back passage.

I staggered down to Piccadilly after this incident. It felt like a graveyard; there was no traffic and no people, not even a mad stranger or some crazy person sleeping in a doorway. I ached and I was bleeding. I went back to Wardour Mews to see if I had imagined the whole rape and to see if I could see this man again. I jumped headfirst over a low wall in the mews just to see whether it was real or not. I smashed my eyelid and my eyebrow wide open. I felt the blood and I felt the pain. I felt something at last. I went to Greek Street Hostel, and they called an ambulance. When my eye was stitched up, I asked not to be given an anesthetic. I felt the needle and the stitching, and I screamed. I needed to experience the pain, to know what was real. Afterward, I went back to Wardour Mews and talked to people who knew the man I described. He really did exist and was known for his cruelty.

For a while I became obsessed with escalators. Once, after taking a lot of barbs, I waited for someone to walk up the stationary middle escalator in a tube station. I went over and peered down, and suddenly I was falling, somersaulting to the bottom. When I hit the ground, I laughed with relief. I went and told the ticket collectors—who at the time used to be at the bottom of the escalator—that I had fallen down, and they didn't believe me. So I went back up and stood peering down again, thinking, *My God, I fell down there.* I could have gone down again.

About this time, I met a young woman called Sheila from Sevenoaks in Kent. Sheila is now dead. She wanted to take care of me, as did many other addicts. Sheila was not liked by those who had been with her in Holloway prison, and I was told that she was with me just for my prescription, but again I didn't care. I had sex with Sheila, and she helped me score barbiturates. She drank cider, and while I lived with her in her squat in Brixton, I started drinking again and couldn't stop. First it was cider, bottles and bottles every night on top of the usual cocktail of drugs. I used to wake up, sweating stale cider, and it made me heave.

Gradually, I moved back on to whiskey. Drink became an essential part of my drug taking. I took to staying in doorways in Leicester Square, sleeping next to Dino, who is also dead now. Dino was a dyke who had a little corner in a doorway opposite the Swiss Center, leading into another street across from the ladies' toilets. She slept here on and off for years. Dino always had a drink and some drugs and an eye to the main chance. She was very lonely.

Dino invited me to sleep beside her, and in the morning she would give me a cap of whiskey to calm the junk sickness. In return I would give her an amp of biseptone. Considering that, at that time, you could sell an ampoule for up to a fiver, that was an expensive cap of whiskey. Sometimes she would give me another capful, and that would be another ampoule. This was getting expensive, so I stopped sleeping there. She came looking for me and begged me to sleep in the doorway beside her, and so I relented. It was a bank holiday and the toilets were open, but the Underground closed earlier. I was very sick, but I managed to get some barbiturates. Dino managed to get a bottle of whiskey.

Some time later I came round, and a Geordie man named Frank, a loose friend of mine who sold paintings and other gear, was standing over me. My head was bandaged. I asked him, "What happened to me?" He told me that he had found me on the steps with my head split open and called an ambulance, which took me away. Dino had disappeared out the back way on to Piccadilly. He was sure that she had hit me over the head with the whiskey bottle. I began to remember the doctor telling me that I had sixteen stitches in my head, and that I ought to stay in the hospital because it was possible I could develop meningitis. I had asked them to give me an injection of biseptone, but they were unable to do this until the morning, so I had left.

That night I was sleeping in the doorway again next to Dino in Leicester Square. I had a silly cap on my head, and the pain was pounding. Dino was snoring in her sleeping bag while I slept between two pieces of cardboard. It was a cool evening, and I felt ill. For a while I dozed off, and then I thought I felt rain, and I licked my lips. I sensed a shadow standing over me, and I looked up and saw a policeman fastening his fly and walking on. I sat up and looked at the clock in Leicester Square, which said 3:45 A.M. I slouched back and thought, *I wonder if he knew I was human?* Where was my rage? For a few months I felt nothing, but then I wanted to kill him and I knew I just had to get off the street.

A couple of nights before this incident, while I was under the influence of barbiturates, I had had my head kicked in by a gay boy because I hadn't shown him enough respect. I knew the violence that was being meted out to me now was a sign of how I had lost *my* respect on the street and how messed up I was. It was time to get off the streets, so I did.

11

THE ONLY OTHER PLACE
IS THE GRAVE

17 July 1995. The last time I was in Robin's room, I spoke about my encounter with Mary in the toilets just after Jean's death, and how all the addicts had passed judgment on me. How could I have loved Jean if I could do this with Jean dead?

One woman had said to me, "Chris, why couldn't you wait a few days? People would have understood more then."

"Do you think I went in there and planned it?" I had answered. "Anyway, I am not accountable to anyone in this toilet. Jean will understand, and if you don't understand, that's not my problem." It was incredible that up until that moment, I hadn't felt any guilt, and

then suddenly I did. After speaking about this with Robin, I went home to the boat.

Yesterday, which was a Sunday, I handed in the keys to the convent, and now it is no longer my home. When I went back yesterday afternoon, my friend who used to live on the boat went into the hospital to have a baby. I found out at seven this morning that she had had a little boy, eight pounds five ounces, at 5:15 A.M. The father, Alex, rang me up, and he was very happy. This is a man in recovery, and I am overjoyed for him. Jean's death and the birth of a baby: the two experiences sit side by side. It is a painful time for me because I didn't honor Jean's death: I left her to lie in the hospital, I never went to see her, I never let her family know.

After deciding to get off the streets, I went to stay at Greek Street Hostel and met Caroline, a woman who worked there. She took me to her room in Camden Town, where I lived with her for just over three years. She was a feminist, as were her friends, whom I met. However, this was not to be the uplifting experience I had often dreamed about, but again one that left me full of shame. I robbed Caroline's friends because I felt they looked down on me. I saw them taking drugs and behaving as I did, but they also seemed to have some control over their lives. They were musicians, writers, politicians, and they led groups to support the Irish Republican Army (IRA). They were able to get on with their lives, so why couldn't I?

In the early days of my relationship with Caroline I became close friends with a toilet attendant in Piccadilly named Betty, who had been very fond of Jean. I actually never paid much attention to Betty until Jean died. Betty was a stocky Glaswegian who wore overalls and curling pins under a head scarf. She was not beautiful, but many of the addicts had great affection and respect for her. She told me that Jean had asked her to take care of me, and that she intended to do so because she had given Jean her word.

When I was stoned and filthy dirty, she would change my clothes and dress me in clean clothes that had been left in the toilet. She would take my dirty knickers home at night to wash and would bring me clean ones to put on the following day. She would try to make me eat when I had come out of Middlesex or any other hospital after overdosing. When the toilets opened early, about 6:30 A.M., she would take me into the little office and cook me toast with an omelet or a scrambled egg. I ate to please her. I borrowed money from her, and in between getting stoned, I would sell some drugs and bring back the money she had loaned me. Hours later, I would go and re-borrow it, and so it went on. Betty *cared* about my well-being, and she truly felt she was helping me by lending me money to score drugs. She didn't know about enabling people to kill themselves.

Betty went to the hospital to have a cancer operation, and when she came back to work she said to me, "You know, Chris, I am just like you now. I'm a junkie; I take more drugs than most of your lot put together. I'm in pain all the time, and there's something seriously wrong with me." Then she disappeared again, and the next I heard, when I came out after another spell in prison, was that she had died in the hospital. They had operated on the wrong part of her; she had cervical cancer, not bowel cancer, and the second operation proved too much. I felt so angry that someone else who loved me, and whom I had loved, had died. Perhaps I was bad news to be around. I felt this anger again later, when Caroline began to get messed up on drugs.

I wanted Caroline to take care of me, which she did. Betty had met Caroline in the toilets when she came to look for me, as she often did, and told me that she was a good person. But Caroline was codependent, addicted to the addict, addicted to straightening me out, which of course wasn't happening. I wanted to get worse. As soon as she came into the flat, I knew where her money was and I stole it. Caroline started wanting me to inject her, and eventually I did. She began to inject herself and slowly started along the path toward becoming a very sick woman.

At this time, I began to feel the need to make friends with an animal, and I decided I wanted a dog. Friends of mine in Carol Street told me about some puppies that were available. I made my way to a house just off the Finchley Road, next door to where Jean and I had lived when we used to collect our prescriptions from Bliss's. When I went inside, all these puppies came flying at me, and the woman there told me to sit down. One little black puppy with a white flash between her eyes down to her nose came over and just looked up at me lovingly. She chose me. I took her back to the house I was sharing with Caroline, where I stayed until my dog was three.

Gradually I got to know my new puppy. Everyone kept giving me names for her, and finally I told them to stop ranting. "Let's call her Maybe," I said. It was perfect for me at that time. Maybe things could get better; maybe I could do something with my life. Maybe and I became the best of friends despite the times she cowered in fear from all the rows that were going on between Caroline and me. Maybe made me laugh, and she took care of me. Maybe and I were to have a relationship for over five years.

Caroline was a very bright woman; she had a degree, she wrote, and there were very few things she couldn't do, except find a reason to live for herself. This was her great challenge, and at times she was close to suicide. She did love me and wanted me to get well, but just because *she* wanted this didn't mean it worked like that. When I didn't meet her expectations, she became angry.

One night Caroline stayed out, and I knew she'd been with a lover. She stayed out again, and this time I knew it was with a man. I went dead inside in the same way I had with Jean over Esha and earlier with my stepfather. I decided to punish her. I stole more and more, I despised her, and one day I threatened her with a bread knife. She looked at me, and I said, "You think I wouldn't do it."

Thankfully she said, "I know you'd do it, Chris."

And it was true. For a moment I saw her lying on the ground with her throat slashed wide open. I threw the knife down and said, "What have I become? What has happened to me?"

Not long after this, I broke into the gas meter and took the money to a pub in Kentish Town. Maybe was with me. I got very drunk and fell on the ground in the pub, and all the fifty-pence pieces fell onto the floor. I was told afterward that Maybe just sat over me and watched me. This was typical of my behavior, and each time I came to, I was remorseful. Then I went right out and did it all over again.

Another time, in a pub where I was well known because Caroline was always coming to drag me out, I found I only had enough for the price of one drink. I went next door to the florist's and found a pile of beautiful roses that had been thrown away. I took them into the pub and offered them to a couple.

"Would you like to buy your girlfriend a bunch of flowers?" I asked.

The man said, "Yeah, how much, Chris?"

"Fifty pence," I said, just enough to get me a drink. Then everybody in the pub wanted them. I sold them all, and I drank and I drank and I drank. As the heat got to the flowers, all their petals fell off. Suddenly all the petals were on the floor of the pub, and everybody wanted their money back, but I had drunk it all away. I had to leave the pub quickly, once more running away from trouble.

When Maybe was over two years old, I mated her with a collie from the Old Farm House Pub in Kentish Town. One night, I came back from a pub and found that Maybe had given birth to six puppies, and more were on the way. I was so proud. I ran screaming and jumping into the street so the whole world would know that Maybe had had pups. I went back to the pub and told them to open the door, and we drank until two in the morning to wet the heads of Maybe's pups. I named each puppy after jazz singers, like Billie Holiday, and Wolf after the Irish freedom fighter. When she was only two days old, the puppy named Billie found her way to Caroline's bedroom and scratched on the door. (Billie is still Caroline's dog.)

Despite having all these pups, Maybe still looked after me and found the time to make me laugh. On the side of her ear she would put silly hats that I used to wear, or snuggle up under my donkey jacket and play with a ball. When Caroline told me off about my behavior and I cried, Maybe would put a paw on me and lick my tears away.

Around this time, a street cleaner found one thousand pounds in a dustbin, so I began looking in dustbins in this area. I found two guns: a .38 Smith & Wesson and a Replica. I didn't know that guns were made of copper or brass, and I didn't know how to use them, although I kept having a go without success, so I tried to sell them.

I went into a pub and showed one of the guns to a couple of men who had been drinking for a while, and they took it into the toilets. It was all very serious business, and when I got home, a man rang and said he would like to buy the gun. He said he'd leave sixty pounds over the bar, where I was to leave the gun wrapped up. I followed his instructions and collected the money. Luckily I didn't blow it, because the man, who was a well-known gang leader, rang back telling me the gun was too stiff and he wanted his money back. I took the gun back and kept it, but I didn't know how to oil it, and I don't think any of these people with all their flash act and talk knew either.

Caroline took me to Ireland. She knew I had always wanted to go there and that one day I vowed I would live there. We went for a three-week holiday and rented a cottage, which she paid for. It stood high on a hill overlooking the Atlantic just outside a small village called Burton Port in Donegal. Naturally, the holiday was colored by my addiction. My clinic in London had contacted one in Dublin so that I was able to pick up prescriptions for methadone to see me through my holiday. After collecting the prescriptions in Dublin, we traveled down to Dunlow and found a chemist. I was told that I would have to pay over one hundred pounds for these prescriptions, and I couldn't afford this. I told the pharmacist that I only had a little money, and he sent me with a note to a doctor in the area who allowed me to have the medication free of charge. I thought that what these people in Ireland had done for me was such a generous thing.

Before we arrived at the cottage, we had spent one night in Letterkenny, where we had gone drinking in the pubs. I was shooting my mouth off about supporting the IRA. My jacket was covered in political badges: "Troops Out," one read; others showed my support for the Armagh Coordinating Committee, which was organized by women to support the women in Armagh Jail; and others showed symbols that related to the hunger strikes. Caroline and I found a bed and breakfast that let Maybe sleep in the room, and I went downstairs to the bar. I was crashing out, almost drunk, and suddenly a man pressed something into my body, and I knew it was a gun.

"I want to talk to you, Englisher," he said. He spoke very softly, and I was very frightened. "Now everybody's been telling me about you in this town. We think you work for the Brits and you've come over to be planted among us to see what you can find out. Why are you so interested in supporting the Irish?"

He could see how drunk I was, and I told him about my love for Ireland and that I was a drug addict. I said I had only recently started going to political groups, and that perhaps it wasn't a good time for me to be involved with politics because I had this desperate problem with drugs. I rambled on, and when I stopped, he put his hand on mine and bought me a drink.

"It's a good job that I interrogated you and not those four men there," he said, pointing them out at the end of the bar. "Those men would have taken you on the moor and tortured you mercilessly, and you might never have lived—you wouldn't have died outright, but you would have died from what they did to you. I'm a different kind of man; I hear that you love Ireland and that you are sincere and you don't work for the British government." I was so relieved.

Before he let me go, he said to me, "Learn a lesson: you do not run around shouting your politics out, particularly in a place like Ireland and particularly if you come from the enemy."

I knew this was real, and I suddenly understood the situation in Ireland far more than I had when I stood on Kilburn High Road, silently supporting the cause of a hunger striker or marching on the London streets.

The pink cottage we stayed in was a two-mile walk down a country lane, past farmhouses down to the ocean. Ireland was as beautiful as I had imagined it would be from the postcards I had seen. I felt at home, and the gypsy-like people picking blackberries down the lane greeted me. Every day I walked the two miles with Maybe up the field, took the school bus to Dunlow, and came back with my script. On the way back, I would have a couple of pints in Burton Port, sometimes more, and then Maybe and I would go back to the cottage where Caroline would be knitting, cooking, reading, or being very quiet. I often felt ashamed that I couldn't just go and get my script without sneaking off to the pub and not admitting it.

Near the pink cottage there was a farmhouse with several cows. One cow had two calves, and Maybe, who had never seen country life before, barked and tried to chase them. The mother cow kept trying to run up this little slope to get at Maybe, who would hide behind a tree, and this went on over and over again. Eventually the cow got up the slope, but Maybe was too fast and got away.

Another time, we were walking through a hamlet of chickens, donkeys, and other animals, and Maybe scattered the chickens. The farmer shouted at me. Then Maybe teased the donkey, who got angry and frustrated because it was tied by a rope. It was well known in the area that there was a city dog around, and the male dogs on the farm liked Maybe and used to follow her to the pink cottage. Some farmers came and banged on the door and ordered me to keep this city dog away from their working dogs or they would shoot her. I knew they weren't bluffing, so I kept her on the lead when we went across the hamlets. If we were walking in the fields to the bus stop, I let her run in the fields and go rabbiting, but she would always meet me just before we got to the road. She would never go too far from me.

Sometimes in Donegal we climbed over the fields and walked down the cliffs to the ocean. Caroline swam, but I didn't have the courage to swim in the sea. I sat on the beach and savored the solitude. I loved the countryside because it was so relaxing and I could be silly with my dog. Caroline cooked lovely meals for me and created an atmosphere of hominess and warmth. She tried to show me a way of life without drugs, but I couldn't explain to her that I had no control over my addiction.

One time we went to Burton Port and met a man who was nearly ninety. He wanted to marry me even though he had never met me before in his life. Another Irishman said, "There you are, Chris, you love Ireland so much, marry him and you'll have a home here, there'll be no problem. You can have your girlfriend with you as well." Everyone knew about Caroline and me, but they didn't seem narrow-minded, although I don't know what they said when we weren't there.

The same day we walked back through a small hamlet where a woman was getting water from a well. I said hello to her, and she said, "Hello, Chris, me and my sisters have been waiting for you to come. We've been waiting for you to come back to Ireland." Caroline asked me if I knew this woman and I replied that I had never met her before in my life. I looked up at the farmhouse and waved back at the two older sisters, who were waving to me and beaming. I said cheerio, and the woman looked at me and said, "You'll be back, you'll be back one day."

I remember saying to Caroline. "See, I told you I was Irish; she knew, she knows I'm Irish." Caroline just thought the woman was crazy.

Not long after we returned from Ireland, I decided it would be better if I left Caroline. One night I waited for the man Caroline was having a relationship with. As he came round the corner of Carol Street, I saw a skewer in the gutter. I said hello to him in a friendly way, and when he came closer, I said, "I'm going to stab you in the balls now; you're never going to screw Caroline again." He was very frightened, and he tried to talk to me calmly, but I ended up stabbing him. I think I caught the top of his thigh, and then I stabbed him again. I just missed his testicle. Suddenly I realized what I was doing and said to him, "I really don't know what is going on with me." And I took Maybe and left.

I wanted to move, so I saw social workers every day, and I cried. I moved to a basement in a shared house in Tufnell Park Road with Maybe. I went into the Catholic church and stole money. I went to the pub and conned drinks. I manipulated money from the pharmacist at the chemist I used in Kentish Town. It seemed that wherever I went, I created trouble. I was a wreck.

I developed an abscess on my upper left leg below my buttocks. I considered myself quite fortunate, because for an addict, an abscess is one way of getting the poison out of the body. The abscess was extremely painful and well advanced. Eventually I had it removed at University College Hospital, and they wouldn't give me any medication because I was a registered addict. I was in agony. I left with a scar eight inches long and about one and a half inches deep. I walked from University College Hospital, just off Tottenham Court Road and Gower Street, to Tufnell Park Road, but on the way I went to the chemist to pick up my linctus. I went to the health center and asked them if they would look at the abscess, and a nurse repacked it for me. I screamed and screamed—I wasn't naturally somebody who cried out with pain, even when I was drug sick. This was raw pain. I had to go twice a day for six weeks to have it cleansed and packed. In between visits to the clinic, I spent much of the time resting, as it was so painful to walk.

I lay in bed in Tufnell Park Road, going over the more beautiful moments I had shared with Caroline. On one of my birthdays, Caroline had taken me to Brighton, and it poured down with rain. I stole money from her that day to go and buy whiskey in the Belvedere Beach Bar. On the pebble beach in the rain, Maybe ran backward and forward, in and out of the water, and she had a great time and we all got wet through. Later, we all went into the Belvedere. So much of my time with Caroline was a mixture of extremes: beautiful memories mixed with destructive incidents, at a time when I was much closer to death than she realized.

After I recovered from my abscess, I moved to a house full of women, most of whom were on parole from prison. I didn't get on particularly well with them. I used to see them drinking and taking drugs, but none of them seemed to be as messed up as I was. The harder I tried to straighten out, the worse I became. My level of hopelessness and desperation was becoming more acute, until one day I playfully pointed my gun at the woman next door, and I thought she was going to die from fear. I didn't understand her response, and she reported me to the housing association.

That evening, I let one of the women who had been thrown out of the house stay with me. She let everyone know she was there, and I was reported. I had broken two rules and owed lots of rent, so I was asked to leave. Once again, I had nowhere to go.

12

THE STOPPING PLACE

19 July 1995. This morning good news came through the post regarding my degree at Oxford Brookes University. I enroll for my master's degree on 30 September, and the course begins on Monday, 2 October. Enclosed in the information pack was a plan for the year ahead, including my chosen subjects and the assessment requirements. This time it is not a pass or fail situation, and I feel that a weight has been lifted from me. I am very keen to start working, and I hope to receive my reading lists soon. It was a good start to an otherwise overcast day. I took the dogs for a walk and, like the animals in the fields, they lacked energy. I, too, felt lethargic, but I continued my commitment to physical fitness and went to the gym.

Later, on my way to Robin's house, I saw a man on Cowley Road dressed in the current fashion, with his baseball cap on back to front, jeans and denim jacket, and sneakers on his feet. He looked unkempt, angry, and quite frightened. He was holding a pile of newspapers in his hand and throwing a sheet at a time onto the pavement. The slight breeze scattered the pages, and soon the pavement was littered up. Somebody called the police, and apparently this man had been seen putting lighted matches into a bin the night before.

A young Asian man shouted at him by name from across the road, calling him a "nutter!"

An angry exchange ensued, with the first man threatening, "I'll punch you in the fucking mouth."

People gathered outside their shops to watch this menacing scene. It was almost as if everybody knew this man was going to attack someone if he wasn't restrained. There was some discussion between one man who thought he was sick and needed help and another who felt that the man knew what he was doing and was making a point, and even if he was sick, he should be allowed to behave as he wanted. I watched the effect that this behavior had on people, and I was shocked and amazed.

One woman with three children stood outside her shop with her husband and said, "Talk about nutters, we're surrounded by them here. We're lucky to be alive."

I stood, watching the stress this behavior caused in other people just trying to go about their lives. For once I was watching someone else causing this, but not so long ago it could have been me.

Finding myself once more with no place to live and no place to go, I went to the pub with Michelle, a friend of Caroline's. I spoke loudly near a woman named Pam so she would hear how desperate I was. Pam and her husband, Bill, agreed to let me stay until I sorted out a place to live. In the meantime, Caroline's new partner, an addict who disliked me and I him, but not the man I had attempted to stab, helped me find a squat. I moved to Hackney with Maybe in 1983, two years before I would finally admit defeat. Toward the end of my using, I became a real threat to other people.

The chemist just off Victoria Park Road in Hackney was closed for redecoration, so I found a chemist a mile and a half away over May Street and beyond London Fields. This meant a long walk, which I did not relish, knowing how sick I could get, but it did mean that Maybe had a daily walk. The chemist was in a tiny village area with two pubs, an electrician, and a butcher, and I quickly became known there because I was often seen vomiting and dry heaving in the streets.

In the winter the snows came. In January, I was up to my knees in snow as I crossed London Fields. I was wet through every time I reached the chemist, and then I had to walk back. I seemed capable of putting myself through any hardship just to get my script. I bumped into people I had known from years before, other addicts from Piccadilly who picked up their scripts at this chemist, and some looked pretty rough. Others looked just the same.

I made friends with the man who ran the electrical shop. I think he was from Jamaica. I told him I lived in a squat and asked him if he would come and fix the electricity. The cases were off the plugs, and one day, stoned, I had been clearing up, and a black bag with a bottle in it had touched a raw wire, causing a flash. I was very frightened because I knew that I did strange things when I was stoned. The electrician came round and brought me a bottle of whiskey. We had sex because that was what he wanted. He told me that if I hadn't been a lesbian he would have married me, which was all talk, but at least I had a bottle of whiskey.

He came several times a week, and I used to go into his shop. He was a married man, and sometimes his wife was in the shop. She would look me up and down with contempt. She knew that there was something going on, and she would ridicule me in front of other women. When the shop was empty, I would nip in through to the back, pretending to go to the toilet. Sometimes I actually went and stole money. Eventually, the electrician realized that every time I was around, money went missing, and he barred me from the shop. I was sorry about that because he was a reasonable man. He had paid me fairly for my services and I had robbed him; again I had no control over my behavior.

After having a drink in a pub, picking up my script, and drinking the methadone, I would walk back over London Fields with Maybe. I had already gotten to know someone who sold sulfate in the area, and I was heavily in debt to her. I had also learned how to manipulate her, and she agreed to let me sell some sulfate in exchange for a fix. I did this for a while, and sometimes when I got some cash together, I paid off part of the debt and got the rest on tick.* But no matter what I did at this time, I was always in debt.

I made "friends" with the owner of Fred's Off Licence. Poor Fred didn't know what to do with me. I wanted him to say no when I wanted booze on tick, but he couldn't, even though I said that I would respect him if he did. He just said that I would talk him out of it anyway. On Sunday afternoons, I used to clean his van for a miniature whiskey and four cans of Special Brew. I always did a good job.

In Victoria Park, Maybe would play and run and swim. I would watch the bowling and became obsessed with it. I began to see what great skill there was attached to this sport. Maybe used to get very annoyed and bark. My days were empty. I would desperately try to do something that would make me feel some sense of satisfaction, but then the day would always be over. After the visits to the park, I would go back and lie on the bed and read Agatha Christie novels. Maybe would look at me appealingly; she knew I was getting closer and closer to death.

Yet I knew no matter how desperate I got, I had to take Maybe out for her walk and feed her. She kept me going. One day when we had no money, but I had had some drink and my linctus, we had only a tin of soup to eat. I said to Maybe, "Well, we can have us some soup, Maybe, but we've got no bread," and she went out and came back with half a moldy loaf. I said to her, "This isn't the kind of bread we want, we want fresh bread," so off she went and came back with more bread, which we ate. No one ever believed me when I told them this story.

My squat became filthy. I had painted the walls all different colors, and I hadn't completed one of the walls. The effort to do any-

---

* credit

thing was beyond me. I became increasingly paranoid and kept a mallet by my bed and a knife under my pillow. Behind the door there were hammers. My paranoia was encouraged by some of the incidents that took place while I lived in Hackney.

There was an African family who lived across the road, and their young daughters used to tease and mimic me, calling Maybe. One of the daughters would hide behind a curtain when Maybe looked up, and she did this repeatedly until Maybe would bark. It went on for ages, and one day I said, "Look, will you stop teasing her, leave her alone."

A large group of men came out and said, "If you don't shut up, we'll kick your fucking dog to death." Something snapped inside me. I walked away and took Maybe up to the house. I started to punch the walls until my fists bled. I screamed, "Maybe, they're not going to use you as a scapegoat. They're not going to hurt you." I knew this was no idle threat.

When I had calmed down, I walked back into the street where nine men were lined up outside, from the oldest, in his mid-forties, to the youngest, a boy of about seventeen. I looked at them all and said, "Look, whether you like what I do or not, it's my life. I am entitled to that kind of respect to live my life. I don't interfere with you when you are stripping your cars down, beating your wives; I don't interfere. I want to be able to live here without your interfering. I don't want you to use my dog as a scapegoat to get at me. I'll tell you something: She's not like the other dogs in the block; she doesn't come round to bite you." Then I said, "Now, there's nine of you, let the first one raise his foot. I don't know if my dog will bite you or not; you're going to have to take that chance. But I won't stand by and watch you do it, so let the first one raise his foot." I wasn't drunk, but I was very frightened.

The men filed away one by one. The father of the daughters turned round and said, "I'm sorry. I apologize."

"Your daughter was teasing and taunting the dog. She doesn't need to do that," I replied, and he just walked away and left me alone.

The chemist reopened near Victoria Park Road, and my journey was shortened. A very well educated African ran the shop. He was concerned about me. He said he respected my intelligence and he couldn't bear seeing people ridicule me. His wife was a doctor in St. Mary's Hospital in Paddington and worked with addicts.

"I don't know how to stop," I said.

"Do you know how ill you are?" he asked.

"Yes I do, I know I am very close to death."

For a few days I would go in there reasonably sober, and he would remark on it. Then I would be off again, too much sulfate or booze.

During this time, I got to know people who used in Hackney, and they knew that I was really messed up. I scored some sulfate one day from a group of lads who were passing by.

"Have you got a needle?" I asked him. "I've got a syringe."

One of them replied, "Yeah, come on, we'll go round to your place."

He, too, was really off of his head, but we went to the squat and when we got there I said, "Have you got the needle?"

"No I haven't," he said and caught hold of me. He was a young man of nineteen and I was a wreck of forty-six years old. He said, "I'm going to rape you."

"Oh yeah!" I picked up the mallet and swung it at his head. I saw the fear in his eyes, and for a moment I could have crushed his skull in, but I relented. Then he swung my arm back and the mallet caught my left knee. He flung me on the bed and ended up raping me.

When he had run out of the flat I was in a state of shock, and I took Maybe out into the street. We passed a policeman who was doing his gardening, and I told him what had happened.

"My God!" he said. "He must have been hard up. Your luck's changed."

"Do you hear what I'm saying?" I said.

"Go away, Chris, everyone knows you're off your head."

So I went to the off license and told Fred, who believed me and asked, "Do you know who it is?"

Every time a man came in I said, "That's him. That's him. That's him." I was really lost.

"Are you sure it happened, Chris?" Fred asked.

"Have you ever heard me talk like that before?"

"No," he said. "You've been in some funny situations with men, but I've never heard you say anything like that." He believed me.

I took Maybe to Pam's, and she agreed to take her for a few days while I went to Tooting Bec Drug Unit. I was there for five days. No one was interested in helping me stop using. I just rested and took my drugs. When I came out I realized that no one in the world gave a damn whether I lived or died. Some kind of anger was kindling in me, a different kind now, about my right to live a life that was not about abuse. I started having fantasies about a different way of life, but the turning point was still a few months away, and in the meantime I got worse.

I became friends with a gay man from Galway named John, whom I met in the off license. He had moved into a flat where the remains of a dead body were rotting away, and he had had to throw them out. I tried to avoid him at first, but eventually we became mates. He used to play with Maybe and paddle in the lake at Victoria Park. Sometimes he would go really deep, and people would look at him as if he were a bit odd. I thought his behavior was fine. One day he made me a meal and it was like human vomit, but I didn't have the courage to refuse it. He told me it was chicken something, and I ate it. Afterward he said to me, "Thank you for eating with me. Other people have just walked out when I've made a meal."

In the mornings I took blood pressure pills that kept me calm until I got to the chemist to pick up the script, even though the chemist was just down the road now. I still woke very early and had to get through the time until the chemist opened; every minute I waited seemed like an eternity, and I was always there about twenty minutes before the pharmacist arrived.

I met a woman named Jean, whom I had known in prison. She was now living in Hackney with her husband, Bill, whom I had heard about and who was always in and out of prison himself. They were staying with an older man who was a friendly alcoholic with a dog, too, and I got to know him from hanging round the off license. Jean used to sell me Valium, and I remember once when she wouldn't let me have any until I had some money. I began to see that there had been a time in the West End when I had had a very good name, because I always paid my debts back. Now times and people had changed. Even those virtues I felt I had in the drug world were disappearing, and I felt more desperate than ever.

I stole a radio from a van belonging to a Maltese gang. If I had been caught, I was told I would have been cut to pieces, and still I flirted with danger. Another time, I spent the whole night, with Maybe beside me, going through dustbins and I found three cassette recorders, which all worked, and lots of books too. I had over two hundred books in the squat, and I loved them. Because I had no money for drink, I sold some books each night at the secondhand shop, and eventually there were no books left. I began to go into empty buildings just before the builders moved in and take up the carpets. I dragged enormous rolls of carpets on my shoulders, hoping to take them home, and then I left them in Victoria Park Road. Sometimes I would find furniture, too.

Michelle was a friend of mine who came over to the squat sometimes. I had given her her first injection when I lived with Caroline. She was Irish and also a dyke. It was good to see her when she came over; we would have a drink and a fix, but then she wandered off. As time passed, I went to visit Caroline and Jimmy, the little boy she had given birth to. Her partner still hated me and I him, but I tried not to be insulting when I went to visit. Every time I left Caroline's, I felt guilty for the way I had behaved toward her, but I didn't know how to put it right.

These months of decline were symbolized by my inability to cope with myself or other people. I was always getting into scrapes of one sort or another. I felt unwanted and unloved. An African woman who lived in the squat had loaned me a pound and always seemed to catch me when I didn't have the money to pay her back. She was a feisty woman with a husband who drank a great deal. She won £1,100 on the football pools, and her husband asked me for the pound the next morning.

I said to him, "You've got some cheek. You've just won all that money and you're asking me for a pound." He told his wife, and later that afternoon she caught me on the landing and gave me a good hiding. I was unable to defend myself.

Afterward, John, my Irish friend, said to me, "Chris, why didn't you hit her back?"

"I didn't know how to." Suddenly I got angry and said, "I'll go and do it now," and I took my jacket.

John pulled me back and said, "Chris, she'll kill you, she's a powerful woman. I wouldn't like her to hit me. I don't think I'd hit her back either."

Jean had a friend in prison who wrote me and asked me to bail him out and let him stay at my address. Ridiculously, I agreed. He was an active alcoholic who decided to go on drugs, and although he was extremely violent, he said he would never lay a finger on me. He brought people back to the flat from the West End and always brought me a fix to keep me sweet. I remember seeing him standing naked, washing his feet in the bath, which was full of pans and dirty clothes. Our life at the squat was really squalid. He was a real user in both senses of the word, and although he said he wasn't embarrassed about me, I could see it in his eyes. Whenever he came in, he would look around the flat and find my fix. But at this time, he seemed to be the only friend I had, so I let him stay.

Maybe was getting really fed up. She started staying away from me and sleeping in the other room, whereas until then she had always slept at the bottom of my bed. I left her sometimes with a man I knew, and she loved going into his flat. He told me one night that he had seen me kick her when I was drunk. I was so shocked, and although I didn't want to believe it, I knew that it was possible, because half the time I didn't know what I was doing.

These incidents hastened my decline, but it was a group of children who stopped me in the street one day that really shook me up. They told me I was dirty. I said to these children, "You look about fourteen years old."

They said, "We are, and you're a very dirty woman."

The shame was killing me. I was disgusting. I was so weak physically that I found it hard to drag myself five hundred yards to the chemist. One morning on my way there, it hit me that I never had gone to college or done my writing. Perhaps it wasn't too late. At forty-seven years old, I didn't really believe it was possible, but I thought there was no shame in losing if I had a go at it. I hadn't even given it a try. But then I went back to the flat after picking up my script, got drunk, and forgot it all. The despair was there, but I just didn't know how to let go of the lifestyle: selling sulfate down in the West End in the pouring rain and the burning heat, dragging unhappy Maybe along with me and picking up drinkers from Kentish Town, anywhere, to keep me company. I was utterly lost.

Michelle came over one day, and I told her about a man who wanted me to sort out his sexuality in exchange for setting me up in business selling heroin. I told her I was tempted but I had to look after Maybe, and I couldn't do that gouching out all the time. Michelle spent the night in the other room and we scored some speed.

On Sunday morning I had no methadone, and I was very sick. I did have some sulfate, but I knew it was no using taking sulfate without something to ease the sickness first. I went into the other room and begged Michelle not to leave me alone. I had never before asked anyone in my life not to leave me alone.

"I've got to go, Chris, this is too depressing here," she said.

It was like death in the flat. I begged her to wait a little longer until I could get an idea where to get some money or some booze. I begged her for more time. Maybe came and lay on the bottom of my bed and I saw how unhappy she was. I knew that I could not get through the day. I knew there had been other days like this, but it seemed none had been so empty, desolate, and endless; I wished that I could just die. Then I thought about what would happen to Maybe. Michelle kept saying she couldn't stay any longer, and I begged her to stay each time she wanted to leave. My knees were aching and my legs had started to kick. I needed some drug—either heroin or synthetic heroin—that would still this terrible withdrawal, and I knew in my heart I could not go through this again. I prayed for guidance and help, and immediately into my mind there came a thought: *put down the drugs.*

I said to Michelle, "I'm going to give up my prescription and I'm coming off all drugs."

"All right, Chris," she said; she had never heard me say this before.

"Can I stay at your house tonight?" I asked her. "I'll come back for my money in the morning and pick up my script, and then I'll ask Pam if she'll look after Maybe until I can come off the drugs. Then I'll see what else I can do." I knew what I had to do, and there was no way I could do anything else.

I still had three packets of sulfate in my pocket, and Michelle had found two or three pounds in her pocket. It was evening now, and we went out and had a pint each. I managed to borrow a couple of quid from somewhere—I might have even begged something in the street—then I went and slept at Michelle's flat.

The next morning, after I had gotten my prescription and my money, I told the man who was staying at my squat that I was leaving, but that if he stayed there, the police lived just over the way and he could be picked up. I said he could do what he wanted with the squat. I didn't take all the methadone, but gave some to Michelle.

I went to see Pam. She didn't really believe me, but she agreed to let Maybe stay with her until I went into the hospital. She let me use her phone to phone the clinic, and they said I could go there the next day.

That night I went out drinking and shared the three bags of sulfate, which I had kept and still not used. It was a miracle: I had never had drugs on my person a day without using them, not even half a day. I celebrated my departure from the drug scene with Michelle and Neil, the drummer who had been Caroline's lover while I had been living with her, the man I had attempted to stab in the testicles. We all had a packet of sulfate, and I slept at Neil's flat.

I got up in the morning and just left. I went to Pam's and collected the few belongings I needed. I said good-bye to Maybe and prepared to leave for Tooting Bec Drug Unit. That was 13 July 1985.

III
DYING AND REBIRTH

13

NO MORE DRUGS!

25 July 1995. It is a beautiful July afternoon. The symbolism and enrichment of the present is not lost to me. I sit beside the river regularly as a form of meditation. The dogs play in the water, and again and again I am aware of an energy that unites all things. This is an energy I was denied access to by my unwillingness to open up to it during the years of my using. Only at the point of my final prayer did something awaken within me. Slowly, I was to become aware of the beautiful nature of things. In the transition period between 11 July 1985 and 24 January 1987, I saw many times the mistakes I had made, and I experienced again the anguish, the sorrow, and the shame. I learned so much in this transition period, and not once did I completely lose hope.

When I entered the drug unit and told everyone I was coming off my prescription, no one really believed me. I looked like a tramp, and they told me so. When I undressed, my underwear was soiled yet again, and I apologized to the nurses who didn't seem to comprehend the shame that I felt. Before I was put on a program of withdrawal, I was given drugs to stop me from having barbiturate fits. My greatest fear was alcoholic fits. I was closely observed, and when I had used up all my prescription, I showed how determined I was to change my way of life. I had used drink and drugs for thirty-two years, and I was frightened to be without medication. The withdrawal from drugs was extremely disturbing. I had acute anxiety attacks and terrible dreams, and I saw things crawling on the walls. When I looked at people, their faces were distorted into the most revolting shapes.

My medication was reduced gradually because, as a chronic addict of so many years, I might have died if this procedure was done too quickly. If at any stage during the withdrawal process I felt unable to cope, I was to let the doctors know, and they would increase the dosage. I found some of the support in Tooting Bec questionable. There was an overall unwillingness to believe that I would succeed, and I felt I was the only one who believed I could do it. The doctors then informed me that if it became too difficult, the home office had assured them I could keep my prescription for life. I told them that I didn't think that was helpful; I wanted to have a chance to live a drug-free life.

The withdrawal took me two weeks. My medication was reduced on alternate days. In the daytime, I played table tennis with anyone who would play with me, and this helped me to relax. As the dosage decreased, my awareness of what was going on round me began to sharpen, and I noticed that drugs and drink were being smuggled into the unit. Those patients with gear would also have a go at the rest of us. One woman who came into the unit, Stephanie, never let me forget that I had given her her first injection. She arrived with a broken leg, and inside her plaster cast she had hidden some Valium. I helped her take the Valium out but said I didn't want any. The following day I had my final dose, and Stephanie began winding everyone up about the Valium she had hidden. Eventually I flipped and threatened to kill her if she didn't give me any tablets. She only had three Valium left in a matchbox and said they were already promised to people, but I grabbed her and forced the pills from her. Stephanie told all the other addicts in the ward, and they turned on me. Some came and told me they were going to beat me up. I grabbed Stephanie, and then the night staff came and the finger was pointed at me. I owned up to taking the pills, but not to bringing them in.

After the Valium incident I began to feel the absence of drugs in my system. I lay on my bed in the ward and felt as though the weight of the world was on me. I hurt and I was angry. I watched two young women coming off drugs, and I said to the psychiatrist, "The pain these women are going through."

"And how much worse do you think it is for you, Chris?" she said. "They're very young, and you've been doing it so much longer, you can't see your own pain." And suddenly I began to understand why I felt so exhausted and needed to lie on my bed so much.

One time I went with another patient and a nurse to get some cigarettes and newspapers for the ward. While I was talking to the nurse, the other patient managed to get a bottle of vodka from the shop across the road and smuggle it back on to the ward. We drank half each. Now that my system was relatively clean, the vodka knocked me senseless, and I collapsed on my bed. I had my breath analyzed, and I still denied that I had had any drink.

When Dr. Treganza saw me, I broke down and cried, and said to her, "I'll tell you, but I'm not telling the rest. Never mind that they could smell it; everybody knew. I don't know why people say that it doesn't smell."

She said to me, "Look, it's not the end of the world. This is what you have been doing all your life, Chris. You've never been able to stop, because when it got difficult, you always ran back to get some more."

I listened to her, what I could hear, and said, "It might not be the end of the world for you, but it feels like it to me. If I can't stay off drink and drugs here, what am I going to be like when I go out? I need to go to rehab. I need to learn about drugs and drink."

"That will be taken care of," she told me. "Do you want your script back?"

"No!"

"Just remember if things get too much, you can have it back," she said.

Life on the ward was tough, not least because of the withdrawing from drugs, but because of the other addicts. There were about twenty on the drug unit, mainly men. It wasn't easy. I often caught most of the resentment that was floating around the ward, and many people were violent. Some didn't want me to get off my prescription because they were confronted with the reality that it was possible to do so. Also, if I became drug free, I was no longer one of them. At this stage it was understandable to slip and slide a little, but many of the addicts still on prescriptions felt I should no longer take any drugs. I felt angry with the hypocrisy when I saw all the smuggling that went on.

I worked in the kitchen, doing the washing up and preparing the supper. Addicts were paid a pound a week for any work they did. Lofty, a man I had always feared on the streets, arrived on the ward and took over control of making the tea. It was a ridiculous power game. Lofty became sweet on a woman named Pat, and when I refused her some tea, he put his fist in my face and said, "Give her the tea or I'll break your fucking jaw." I was scared and so I relented. When I went into the kitchen later to make a cup of tea for myself, Lofty poured the hot water over my hand and it blistered.

Later he went and asked Pat for a sexual favor, and the whole ward turned against him. I had warned Pat that if she became friends with Lofty in exchange for drugs, he would want something in return, but she had refused to listen. Lofty felt ashamed, and suddenly I felt sorry for him and sat by him to show that he wasn't there for everyone to have a go at.

He turned round and said to me in front of everyone, "I've had you wrong for years, Chris. I'm sorry I threatened you. You give Pat a fucking hiding if you want. You've got my permission."

I told him, "I don't need your permission, Lofty. I'm sitting next to you to give you some support. That's all I'm doing, because I understand what you're going through." A few days later Lofty signed out of Tooting Bec and went back on the streets.

Michael, an African social worker, showed me the greatest support at Tooting Bec and had some insight into where I was coming from. He told me that one of the addicts he worked with had wanted to go to the drug rehabilitation center, and it had taken Michael ages to find somewhere to place him. In the end, the addict despaired and killed himself. I told Michael that rehabilitation was my only chance. Michael was leaving his job, but he promised to place me in a rehabilitation center before he left. I hung on to this hope.

Michael kept his promise and he took me to the Ley Community in Oxford. On the way to Oxford, the train stopped at a station, and Michael gave me some money to go out and buy some cigarettes and a soft drink. I looked at the whiskey and I nearly gave in, but I just got tea and something for Michael. I had passed his test, and Michael told me he was pleased.

When I arrived at the Ley Community I was questioned by a young Scottish woman who worked there. I knew that she had used drugs. I said to her, "I'm forty-seven years old. You might think that I'm past it, that there are other people who are more deserving."

"Don't do my thinking for me," she replied. I thought, *Thank God there's some straight thinking here.* "You'll get your chance here," she went on. "We're going to discuss it and we think you deserve your chance."

Michael said good-bye, and I never saw him again.

At the Ley Community there was weight training and table tennis, my favorite. There were forty people in the first phase of this rehabilitation from drug addiction; of these, six were women.

I was faced with the wreckage that I had become, physically, mentally, and spiritually. The community consisted of a big house, and there was a river that ran within the ten-acre grounds. It should have been quite simple to find my way around, but when I turned round I didn't know where I was, which room was the dining room or the laundry room, and this went on for weeks. I was affectionately called "Shot Away Wilkinson," and I hated it.

I had endless amounts of time to fill. How would I ever get

through a day? Our days were organized by mealtimes, tasks, and meetings. At the first meeting after breakfast, a house leader would suggest a few items of particular interest relating to the running of the place, and then there was some socializing, maybe some game-playing, like throwing a cushion at each other to help us unwind. At first these games made me twice as tense. For my first task, I worked with the cleaning gang responsible for polishing surfaces. I loathed it and I kept finding any excuse to have a cigarette—I chain-smoked and was told there were only certain times we could smoke. We had meetings after lunch, too, with facilitators who encouraged us to confront each other to help us say what we needed and wanted to. I felt I didn't have the confidence to do this. We had a complaints box, where we could put down our thoughts about certain people and then confront them in the groups. I had a great ability to listen, and I heard the house leader say on my first night there, "If people here listen, they will learn." I listened actively and learned a great deal. I also learned that no one expected me to stay drug free.

By the time I had been there for three months, I had become the manager in the gardens, but I didn't have a clue how to give directions to others or how to organize the gardens, so I did many things wrong. I was also made administration manager, and this infuriated some people because it meant I was responsible for paying wages to certain residents and dealing with receipts. Some of the men really thought they were a cut above me. They were heavy, macho men with very bad prison attitudes, which I had had myself. If I didn't have everything just right, they gave me a hard time. I worked with a man named Larry, who had a degree. He was highly indignant that he was the assistant manager of administration. He tried as hard as he could to undermine me and find fault with my work. Eventually I knew I couldn't work with him anymore, and we had a row in the group. But I still didn't have the confidence outside of the group to tell him to give me a break, and I ended up apologizing to him.

Just before Christmas, when I had started working in the kitchens, I asked for some money from the administration for some shoes. With the money I was given, I bought some shoes and had a couple of quid left over. By now I was fed up with everyone talking about their experiences on the streets, and I felt that some people didn't really know the real horrors of addiction. I felt like a freak. I was the oldest by at least ten years. When I got back to the community, I tried to give the change back, and after looking for the right person to give it to, I decided to keep it. I decided to have a drink or a fix.

That night we went to the pantomime in Oxford as a Christmas treat. I went to the toilet and left by the emergency exit. I sneaked to the bar next door and ordered a double whiskey, then returned to my seat and enjoyed the pantomime. On the way back, the house leader, a very beautiful Italian man named Sebastian, kept looking at me and said, "Where did you go, Chris?" He could smell the booze, so I owned up. He said, "Well, thank you for telling me. I could smell it all through the show. I don't want you to speak to anybody. I will sit with you, and when we get back, you will go straight to your room and I'll phone Louise."

In the morning, I was frightened. I didn't want to be sent away. I had no home, I didn't know anybody who would really want to put me up, and I knew that I wasn't capable of staying drug or drink free on my own.

Louise, who had interviewed me on my arrival, came in very early and said, "I'm not putting you in front of a general meeting." Actually I would have preferred that. I didn't know how to deal with this gentle treatment. Anyone who had used while at the community had been put in front of a general meeting where it was decided whether they stayed or went. "You'll sit on the bench and we'll have a meeting of the staff, and they will decide whether you stay. If you stay, you'll go on contract."

A working contract was an alternative to punishment. It was a period that gave you some space with your feelings and thoughts, which you then recorded in an exercise book to be read by the workers. You were under the charge of another resident and had to do what they told you. You weren't allowed to speak or eat with other residents without permission. The contract lasted for as long as it took the staff to see a change in your attitude.

The first job I had on this working contract was to wash up all the dishes and utensils in the kitchen from each meal. I also had to sweep the leaves down the long drive, possibly half a mile in length. I had to spring-clean the bathrooms as well. I felt that I was working too slowly. There was a big fire in the fireplace of the residents' sitting room, and it always looked so homey while I was on contract. It was a great sense of warmth that I was excluded from. This was a condition of my life, always out in the cold. I stayed on contract for eleven days.

On Christmas Eve I was called to the hall house, and Paul, the assistant director at that time, asked me if I would like to join the community for Christmas. I told him that I would. Then he said that they had agreed I could have Christmas Day off contract, but would go back on for Boxing Day.

On New Year's Eve the community went on holiday to a lovely log cabin in Gloucestershire. There were lots of rooms, and we slept upstairs and cooked downstairs. I knew people were drinking and having sex. I had my period at this time and felt really miserable. Paul tried to make everybody a part of the community, and he thought that I would be cooperative. He said to me in front of everyone, "With your looks and your personality, you're quite lucky to be here; it's not surprising that you couldn't find anywhere else." I just looked at him and wondered why he was being so cruel and unnecessarily personal.

Shortly after this comment, a man delivered some food. I asked him to give me a lift into Gloucester because I had to go on an errand. On the way to Gloucester, I did a bit of fumbling around and said, "My God! I've come without any money. Can you lend me the fare to Oxford please? Give me your address and I will return it to you." I made sure that we had come about eight or nine miles and he was on his way home so we couldn't go back. He stopped at his home and came out with the money.

The first thing I did in Gloucester was get a drink, and then I caught a bus. I didn't know where it was going. As I got on the bus, a car arrived with a worker and two residents, one of whom was my friend Fiona. She was crying and said, "Please come back, Chris."

"No, I'm going to London to see my dog, Maybe," I said. "None of you understand how much I miss her."

I ended up at a police station somewhere, and when I asked them to give me my fare to Oxford, they refused. I asked them to phone Oxford to tell them that I was stuck there. Steve, at the Ley Community, told me I had to find my own way back. I did some begging, went and had a drink, and then jumped on a train to London. The confidence came straight back—I was going to survive, I was going to get some drugs and see my dog. And even though I knew I was lying, I pushed these feelings away.

I stayed at Pam's overnight, where I saw Maybe. I borrowed some money from Pam and went out and got drunk. I rang Paul and told him I was stuck in London, and that I had made a big mistake and wanted to come back. He told me he knew I would ring, and agreed to take me back, but I would have to go on contract.

When I got back, I discovered there were sixteen other people on contract after the shenanigans in Gloucestershire. Some of the women had been having sex, which was not permitted at this stage of rehabilitation so that people could focus on getting sober and clean. Those of us on contract had to clear the grounds, and it was an ordeal. I had to work with Larry, the man who had undermined me so much. We were to dig a trench across a field where a pipe was to be laid. We had to dig two feet wide and two feet down and lay the grass sod on the side because it was going to be replaced. Halfway across, Larry went sick, and I was left to complete this job alone. He then returned for the rest of the contract, which was to empty the swimming pool with a bucket attached to a piece of string. This took days. As the weather changed and warmed up, Paul let me come off contract.

I was now in the second part of my rehab training, but I still felt raw, strange, confused, and in need of something to fill the emptiness within me. I started to go to a fourteenth-century church in Yarnton in search of spiritual fulfillment. I also found the name of a women's group in Oxford and stole some money from the community to go there. But when I arrived, no one was there.

After eight months at the community, I was allowed to drink socially, and so I sat in a pub in Oxford and found my way right back into the company of a couple of alcoholics. One of the men suggested sex, which he paid for. When we went outside the pub to find his bike, I knocked him flying in the alley and took his wallet. I took a cab back to the community and told them what I had done. The next day I was told I could leave if I wanted to, and so I said I would. The director, Brian, tried to persuade me not to go, although many of the other staff members thought I was wasting my time by being there. I had sold barbiturates to Brian in Piccadilly many years before.

I found my way to Tottenham Court Road and had a fix of palfium and Ritalin. I was out of it in seconds because I did a main line, and I lay flat on my back in the toilets. Linda, a lady who drank with me in Kentish Town, said, "If you don't get up and get out, Chris, I'll get the police." Her voice sounded a long way away. I couldn't get up—I was stoned—but eventually I crawled to my feet. When I got up the stairs, Linda said, "Chris, why did you come back to London after you'd gotten off drugs?"

I could hear the puzzlement in her voice and I heard my slurred voice say, "It was like a magnet. It was like a magnet."

14

THE FREEING PLACE

27 July 1995. Today in Port Meadow I drank in the scenery thirstily, and I thought about attitudes toward life in the city and life in the country. Although Port Meadow is in the heart of a city, it has quite a rural atmosphere. Yes, I did find beauty on city streets, but it is a stark and arid beauty full of frenetic movement—an addictive beauty. Here there is a soothing beauty that heals me. It is a strange society that advocates drugs for its citizens and settles for addiction as a way of life. When I was using drugs, it was a criminal offense, frowned upon and unacceptable; now it has become an acceptable phase of adolescence, and this has to be wrong. A society that is blind to its own addiction is a society that cannot see an alternative. I hear now that by the year 2000 the odd ones out will be the children who don't take drugs. There are more agencies for addicts now than ever before, supplying needles, syringes, advice, counseling. There is money-making all over the place, voluntary work to be had, an industry emerging almost on the same level as the pharmaceutical industry, but not yet quite so powerful. Society provides pills for headaches, pills to go to sleep, potions for this and potions for that, instead of looking for the causes and facing the reality of what is done to people from birth. I am extremely alarmed at what is going on. It is a war against people's right to live a free life, another way of control, just like religion has been.

I was back in London and straight into the drug scene. I stayed at Pam's house, but Maybe didn't want to know me in the same way she had before. Pam had fed her ice cream and Mars bars to treat her after all the stress she had put up with from me, and she was really fat. Pam's father had died, and her elderly mother was staying with her. There was lots of drink in the house from the funeral. I slept in the room where the drink was, so it goes without saying that I nicked* some of it. Not only that, one day I stole Pam's Valium and money from Pam's mother's purse, and I went out and got drunk. I had the nerve to go back later, but Pam had called the police and I was arrested. I was told never to go near the house again, although I did eventually return some of the money to Pam's mother. I was thrown out of the police station and told that I was lucky I wasn't charged.

I signed up for unemployment, got a doctor and signed up for sickness benefits, and found a hostel—St. Barnabas in Greek Street. From that hostel, I went to a hostel in Victoria run by the Church Army. This was a very strange place. There were dormitories of women of all ages, but they all seemed ancient, lost, and institution-alized. When my unemployment money came through, it was over two hundred pounds, and I was off scoring sulfate, taking drugs, and drinking. One day I heard the man in charge of the hostel say, "Chris Wilkinson, she's troublesome, manipulative, and dishonest."

---

* stole

Some of the women who worked there tried to convert me to Christianity. I couldn't understand why they couldn't see the regard I had for them; they only saw the things that I did wrong. I was eventually asked to leave the Church Army hostel.

Shortly after, I was arrested for robbing a van in Paddington, where I found what I thought was a big container of money, but which turned out to be a large block of hash. I thought I would be sent to prison with my record, as I had had about thirty-six convictions, all drug related. As the police filled in the forms, I grabbed the hash and tried to swallow it. At the same time, I thought, *I'll go crazy if I swallow this,* so I spat it out. I said to the policeman, "Look, I took this from the van, but I didn't find out what was in the container because you caught me. I thought it was money because it rattled." The court ordered me to stay at a hostel and get a probation report, which I did.

At Rathbone Place Probation Services, I met a probation officer named Dave. He was a Buddhist, and apart from Michael who led me to the Ley Community, he was the first person to understand my deep desperation to become drug free. He told me that if I went to the Fellowship of Narcotics Anonymous (NA) and Alcoholics Anonymous (AA), and showed that I was willing to do something about my problem, he would write my probation report—which he did.

I went to Marylebone Magistrates' Court, and it was the first time I had heard a magistrate speak to me with respect. He wished me well and gave me a year's probation. I begged Dave to help me to stay clean for that year. I knew that if I could get through that year, I would be on my way to recovery. Dave said, "Chris, it's up to you now; go to meetings. I can only make suggestions; I can't keep you from using drugs."

I did go to meetings, and though I was still using drugs, I had stopped drinking. I went back to St. Barnabas Hostel, where I stayed in bed every day. It was the most desperate way of non-living, and I loathed it. When some money came through again, I went to the pub, and while I was drunk I found lots of tools in a van. I started running around the streets of Soho waving hammers and screwdrivers, and when I got back to St. Barnabas, I ran amok with a hammer. I didn't harm anybody, but I was ordered out. There I was again back on the streets.

Dave arranged for me to get into a treatment center called Broadway Lodge in Weston-super-Mare. In the meantime, I had to have somewhere else to stay. The next hostel I stayed at was a resettlement place at 4 Birkenhead Street, King's Cross. It was a very low place, and I had been turned away from it when I was living on the streets.

Eventually I set off for Broadway Lodge. Before I reached Bristol, I stopped and had a drink. I had my fare and some extra money, and Dave had said it was up to me what I did with it. He said there was a place for me at Broadway Lodge if I wanted it, but if I didn't get there, I would be in breach of my probation.

I arrived at Broadway Lodge—a beautiful house set on luxurious grounds, two-thirds of the way up a hill—and rang the bell. Two men came to the door, one of whom I knew from the streets, and a handsome Greek guy who put his arm around me and said, "Do you want to get clean?"

"Yes I do," I said and started to cry.

"Yes, I know you do. Have you been drinking?" he asked.

I said, "Yes, I've had a couple of pints."

"Well, never mind, you've gotten here." It was really nice to be greeted in such a friendly way.

Broadway Lodge is a Twelve Step treatment center which believes in the disease concept of alcoholism and addiction. It uses the Twelve Steps of Alcoholics Anonymous and encourages addicts to talk about their chemical dependency. The first six weeks at Broadway Lodge take people up to Step Five, which is a clearing out of their past life. After this comes extended care, a year-long stay, during which people continue on the Steps but also learn how to live within the community. Most people leave after the first six weeks; some people go on to extended care or other places like halfway houses.

I was put in group three, which was mainly made up of alcoholics. I was quite upset about being put into this group. I wanted to be in the younger group where the addicts were. I didn't like the people around me; they all looked wrecked and faded. I discovered later that many of them had problems facing people like me, with my scarred arms and my street way of speaking, and that they didn't want to be in this group either. Out of this group I know of at least three people who have committed suicide.

The group was made of all classes and social types. I met Tony, a solicitor who was really limited by his superior attitude. He joked about his drunken behavior in front of his family, and he couldn't see that this was a bizarre way to live compared to the lifestyle he represented. Tony was the opposite of me in many ways, with my complex position of inferiority, but we were of assistance to each other. Tony wanted me to be his friend. I told him that I wasn't his friend and that I was there to recover.

There was a woman called Mo in our group, whose husband was a doctor. She believed that she could never measure up to him, so she took drugs and drank to try to be the perfect doctor's wife. Of course she fell flat on her face most of the time. Mo cried and cried and took pills and cried. She was given permission to cry, and I was amazed to discover that some of this crying had to do with frustration and anger. I recognized that some of the tears that I had shed in the past were from anger, and I cried too.

As well as attending meetings, we also had tasks to do like emptying ashtrays and vacuuming. Most of us had done these tasks at some time in our life, and it was no problem for me. But at Broadway Lodge there were millionaires and even royalty, who thought these menial duties were beneath them. Tony tried, but at times it was all too much. It was heartbreaking to see people try to break out of their conditioning and be on an equal level with others.

Group three was a strong group. I wasn't fooled by any of these people; it was as if the veil had been taken from my eyes. I was told afterward that what I saw in other people was also in me. I had been on the receiving end of some of this behavior, so I was familiar with it. I was afraid I might react the same way I had in the past. I noticed that the way I operated in the group was to attack. A merchant sailor in the group, a very beautiful man from Wales, told me, when we were doing our Step One, that he would cross the street to avoid me, and that he only spoke to me in the treatment center because there was no alternative. I told him I knew this, and he seemed surprised that I wasn't offended. I explained that we were both in the same group for similar reasons—in other words, he had no reason to look down on me.

Step One is admitting my powerlessness over chemicals, alcohol, and drugs, and that my life has become unmanageable. Part of the process in the treatment center was to share examples of powerlessness and damage. At the end of the second week, over the weekend, I wrote my life story and took it to the group on Monday. There was always a facilitator in the group who tried gently to get people in touch with their feelings. He wasn't present when we did our life stories because only the group was to respond, but he was there to hear the feedback and to support me or whomever else's life story was being told that day. It was horrific. I told my story in a cocky way, the only way I knew how. People answered questions about the negative and the positive aspects in my life story and wrote a summary including their opinion and their experience of me so far in the treatment center.

A few days later the group reassembled to give me the feedback. One man had written, "Why didn't you get a gun and blow your brains out?" It had been crossed out, but I was still given all the notes after the session. The man apologized for being so judgmental, but it was how he felt. He thought that I hated men, but he hadn't really heard what I had been saying. The feedback from the group was that this was a horror story, and they didn't know how I'd survived. Most people thought I was extremely self-centered and that the universe did not revolve around me. They thought I had been dishonest, and that part of my problem was the heavy burden of guilt and shame that I carried. I clung on to the positive feedback about my willingness to recover, my willingness to help other people, and my honesty to get it all out in the open and to use the group.

Before I moved on to Step Two, I was left in limbo. I had secretly known that my life was horrific, but I had never thought that other people would agree with me. In the past, other people had said I carried a chip on my shoulder or that I made things bigger than they were. I needed to grasp some hope from somewhere because I felt that within me death was taking place.

Step Two is coming to believe a power greater than myself can restore me to sanity. The power for me at the time was this ravaged group of people who were all working toward the same end—a drug-free and drink-free life. I listened and paid attention, and for the first time in my life, I admitted openly that I didn't have all the answers. I didn't know how to live. I had lived through fear and shame. I realized that unless I released the resentment toward my stepfather, who had been dead for over thirty years, I didn't stand a chance of recovery. I also had to forgive my mother. I wrote a grieving letter to my stepfather; it sufficed, but it was only a start.

Most of the counselors at Broadway Lodge were in recovery themselves, and they spoke to us in the mornings. They all had different kinds of addiction. One of them, a brilliant counselor, just said that her life was unmanageable and that she was always in a hurry. There was a sixty-one-year-old woman from Yorkshire named Jessie, who spoke about grieving. When I heard her speak about grieving, I knew that I had to give myself a chance to grieve, to experience those powerful emotions that I had run from most of my life. I suddenly felt reassured.

Before I began Step Three I was assigned a counselor named Brian, a young man who was five years in recovery. He did not like my anger, and the first time I went to see him, I talked about sexual abuse on the streets. I thought somehow he would know that this was me trying to deal in a crude way with my shame, but he didn't. On the streets, when he had been an addict, he had interfered with women who were stoned. He was a very gentle man, but I wasn't really sure about him. Because I had no self-worth and really could not protect myself, I stayed with him as a counselor. However, this was taken out of my hands when he went away.

Step Three is making a decision to hand my will and my life over to the care of God as I understand God. My next counselor was an alcoholic, and he told the story about Charlie, a caterpillar who gets stuck in a bottle of booze and dies. He sent me to the top of the hill to do Step Three. My understanding of God was very confused. I was very frightened before I went up the hill, and I asked many people about Step Three.

Marilyn from Bristol, who I knew had been in treatment before and had had a relapse, said, "Can you think of any reason why not to hand your will and your life to a loving power?"

Like a child, I said, "No." It sounded so clear. But after that the doubts came back.

I went and saw Mary, an American counselor, and I said, "Look, I know this is all very silly, but I'm scared. This making a decision and handing my will and life over is a big step for me. It's reclaiming something that I rejected many years ago. I really have no idea of a loving God."

"Yes, it is scary, I have big problems with it myself," she said. "Chris, this is the step of faith and trust; it's taking a chance. You don't have a problem with taking a chance."

"I don't know about that. I feel very cautious."

"You weren't too cautious on the streets. You took anything and everything." I laughed, and then she said, "Did you ever drink something in a drink and not know what was in it?"

"Oh, often," I replied.

She went on, "Did you ever fix stuff when you didn't really know what it was?"

Again I replied, "Often."

"You got bags of stuff from people on the streets, and you didn't know what was in that sometimes."

"Brick dust."

"That's right," she said. "Take a chance. This might not be brick dust, it might be the real thing. Give it a try."

I went up the hill on a Saturday afternoon. I sat on a huge mound, and I was surrounded by horses and covered by the sky. I felt very close to the sky. There were a couple of farmhouses that seemed to rest below in the dents of the earth. I could see the sea down below me and the sun shining on the water. The sun sat under a big, black cloud, but I recognized its rays reaching the earth and the sea. To my left was a clear, blue sky with white clouds, and down below were all these houses set out like a toy city. Everything was ordered and measured from this distance. I was on the hill looking at all this, and I handed my will and my life over. I saw the roads that led into and out from the town and some that wound down to the sea, and I thought, *There is always a path leading to and from places.* I felt that I could become a part of this life. I saw that I had been extreme in my behavior, and my fear was that I would swing too much the other way. But I also saw there was a chance for me to become Chris. I just stood up, prayed "thank you," and walked past the horses back down the hill to Broadway Lodge.

A man arrived from Bristol, a man who had drunk all his life, and he was put in our group. He thought he was a pugilist, or that was his reputation. He got on my nerves because I had mixed with so many like him before. I had been beaten up by them too. He was almost fifty and wore extremely tight-fitting trousers, and I said I found this offensive. He asked me, "Does it turn you on?"

I replied, "I find it quite revolting that a man of your age needs to strut his manhood in this way, and actually, it tells me a lot about you."

"But what about those women with miniskirts . . ." and off he went.

He was extremely abusive to women in the group, especially older women, but he wasn't allowed to get away with it. There was a young man in Broadway Lodge who was always flirting with the women, and this man from Bristol didn't understand why the young man got away with it when he couldn't. In the end they all talked about how randy they felt. He was pissed off, so he packed his bags, went back to Bristol, and started drinking. A couple of people left after him. This showed me how I also had followed other people's behavior patterns and used situations as excuses to behave irresponsibly.

Broadway Lodge was an intense experience. No stone was left unturned. We were shown films of abused children and the effects of abuse. There were separate groups for men and women who had suffered sexual abuse as children, and very few people were willing to admit it. I mentioned that I had been abused and said, "Let's cut the crap. Don't tell me that none of you has been abused. I feel really disappointed that I have taken this risk, and what you are actually doing is saying, 'Poor old Chris.' You're not saying what happened to you." I was surprised to find that I was able to be more honest than others. I had sunk so low, almost to the grave, and I felt that there was no time to mess around.

Step Four is a fearless and thorough moral inventory of myself. I was given ten days to do Step Four. We used the seven deadly sins as a model. Although I had already done my life story, this was much more difficult, but I completed it. I was able to laugh at some of the absurdities of my life, although I was confronted with my strange behavior that only served to work against me. I didn't know how to value myself. Even when I put myself up, I was waiting for others to knock me back down again.

Step Five is admitting to God, myself, and another human being the exact nature of my wrongs. This took me ten hours to do. I sat in a room, and a woman I did not know listened. Every so often I would say to her, "Is this too much for you?" She had done Step Five many times, and she explained to me that her role was not to judge but to be a vehicle between me and God. After I finished Step Five, I was exhausted. My relationship with my mother had dominated this step, and the incredible punishment that I had meted out to her. I don't think I have ever been in touch with such an amount of pain in one fell swoop. But because this was a treatment center and there was loving support around me, I was safe. I also could choose to run out the door and get a fix if I wanted. Finishing Step Five meant I had completed part one of my recovery at Broadway Lodge.

15

THE SAME MISTAKES

28 July 1995. I walked my dogs this morning. It was a hot and humid day, and the river was quiet. We met Shennon, a beautiful deerhound that Dancer enjoyed racing with. It was lovely to see the dogs bounding around with such energy. After a meal, I went to the convent, where I am doing some temporary work in the kitchen because I need the money. On the way I saw a car knock down an alcoholic man I call Jock on the corner of Manzil Way and Cowley Road. A man got out of the car, pulled Jock by the arm off the road and onto the pavement, and proceeded to get back into his car. Suddenly people arrived from all over the place.

I said to Jock, whose pupils were enormous, "How do you feel?"

"Bloody awful," he said.

"Do you want me to get you an ambulance?"

"No I do not."

"Where do you hurt?"

"My back hurts."

Then a big man came over and took control, and several street people arrived, angry at Jock being dragged off the road with his back hurt. Some younger men came over and supported the driver. People were angry because, they said, you never pull anybody off the road when you've hit them.

"Did you hit him?" I asked.

"Yes, he hit him," a witness said. "I saw the car hit him."

Another witness said to the driver, "You heard from his own mouth his back was hurt when the car hit him. So why did you move him after you'd hit him? You could have killed him by moving him."

The men who supported the driver said, "All right, all right, he didn't know," and pushed the driver into the car.

"Get the car number," I said to someone.

Someone else asked the driver, "Are you going to drive off and leave this man?"

But he didn't, he stayed. Then I went. I heard the ambulance come, and I just moved away because I didn't want to be caught up in all this. It was too familiar, this great show of friendship from street people, which seems sincere. But where were they when this man was staggering on his own across the road? Everyone arrives a little late on the scene and professes undying friendship, and if I sound cynical it is with good reason.

I turned into Leopold Street, and I saw a man sitting on some steps. "Hello, lass," he said.

"Hello, lad," I replied.

"Have you got a cigarette?"

"No I haven't, I've stopped smoking."

"Well, will you go and buy me some?"

I said, "Come on, lad, who do you think you're talking to? Don't try and con me like that."

"Well, I want a cigarette."

"Well, I won't be buying you any."

Part of me wanted to give him some money for cigarettes or a drink or whatever, and part of me thought, no, I'm not going to do it just to silence my guilt. *So I walked away. Maybe it was wrong to refuse this man help, but I remembered that when I begged cigarettes, it was just to get a cigarette, and as fast as I smoked it, I was begging another one. I just thought,* I cannot encourage this man's way of life, that is not going to help him. Neither can I sit in judgment. What can I do? *And so I suppose I took the easy way out, I walked away.*

After completing Step Five, it was suggested that I go to extended care, which was a halfway house at Broadway Lodge. After Step Five, everyone in Broadway Lodge wanted to know how you felt, because people thought that all your problems were solved, but that wasn't the case. Some of my past had been eased, and sharing experiences with the group and counselors certainly lifted some of the burden. I no longer carried my mother's shame and my stepfather's hatred consciously. I told people I felt a sense of achievement. It is no small thing to travel through a lifetime of experiences such as mine and share the exact nature of my wrongs with someone in a room for ten hours. I see now it is a thing of courage. People knew that where I came from, few people stayed in recovery; but I knew there weren't many more chances for me, if any.

A couple of days after doing Step Five, a resident in Broadway Lodge is given a medallion at a leaving ceremony. The whole of the community stands in a circle, and each resident gives something to the person who is leaving. They say what they like about them; usually it is positive, but sometimes the messages are mixed. At the ceremony, there was a beautiful and wealthy woman from Iran named Shusha, who decided that I should dress up and look what she considered feminine. She had beautiful clothes. I had never worn beautiful clothes in my life. She dressed me up in a green silk suit and did my hair, and she insisted that I wear makeup. She applied it with great skill so I didn't look like a clown. She loaned me some beautiful earrings and some very expensive shoes, which she told me had cost her two hundred pounds. Dai, a Welshman, was going to present me with my medallion in the presence of forty residents.

I walked in, and my appearance took everyone's breath away. I felt quite proud of myself. At the same time, I didn't feel like Chris; I felt like a sophisticated woman in this outfit, and I walked and held my head differently. Dai began by introducing the ceremony and giving me the medallion, which was a circle minus a third. It was like an old-fashioned penny, but heavier. On one side it said, "Broadway Lodge," and on the other side it said, "I am responsible." It was an object of great pride for me, something at last that I had achieved. I wasn't sure of the whole significance of the missing piece. Some people said we left part of ourselves at Broadway Lodge, but I looked on it as finding that part of myself that was lost. Because of our damaging experiences, most of us who went to Broadway Lodge felt incomplete. Making the circle complete was what my recovery was truly about.

Everyone formed a circle around me, and most said very beautiful and positive things to me. Some laughed, particularly some of the men who commented on my appearance and thanked me for taking the time and the trouble because they knew this wasn't the way that I presented myself. They also knew how vulnerable I felt in this outfit, and they were extremely supportive, especially the younger men. They seemed intuitively to understand the great difficulty I had in walking into that room. I actually felt like a drag queen, and my high heels were killing me. Dai eventually gave me a hug, and then it was my turn to make a short speech, thank people, and go round and hug every person in the group as a farewell. I had something to say to each individual as I hugged them, and I felt a great sense of belonging.

That was the highlight of my time at Broadway Lodge, but within six weeks I would be back on the streets buying drinks in Paddington with money I had stolen from Broadway Lodge.

After my ceremony, I moved to extended care to interact with society, but within the safety of Broadway Lodge. Extended care consisted of two houses in Weston-super-Mare that were just beyond Broadway Lodge. The houses were quite large. There were offices in one and a large community room in the other, and people slept in both houses.

It became clear to me that I was unable to change several things about myself: one was a great fear of my dishonesty with money, and the other was that I did not know how to deal with resentments. I tried and learned—you pray for the person you resent, you clear your mind of this energy that poisons your system—even so, my self-worth was very low.

Step Six is to become entirely ready to have God remove all my defects of character, and Step Seven is to humbly ask God to remove my shortcomings. I encountered a great deal of prejudice in the group in extended care. I was told that I had an obsession with a woman in the group named Marilyn. I allowed them to tell me what my thoughts and feelings were, and I began to believe what I was told. I didn't particularly like Marilyn or a friend of hers named Theresa, but everyone believed I did.

I worked in the kitchen with several men and made lots of mistakes, but it was fun. We made a daily report of significant events, which we read back in the group the next day. Then I did the laundry in the bedrooms, and became the housekeeper, which meant I held the money for the food, washing, and everything that was bought for extended care.

I did the shopping for the houses in the supermarket with Marilyn and other people. Marilyn was extremely contemptuous of my inability to handle this situation. She had been a social worker and was a very organized woman. I used to wonder what the hell she was doing there, but like me she was a wreck underneath all the efficiency. She could only see other people's faults, and it angered me because I felt so much shame. Then I thought, how could I know how to do all this stuff when I've spent most of my time out of it, or when I've only done it when I've been drunk or stoned?

There were about twelve of us in extended care, both men and women. There were two people I got along with, including a woman named Arabella. She was a very beautiful woman who became friendly with a fellow named Blandford. There was something very nice between us, but she seemed to change in extended care. I had another friend, who had a horse, and she got hassled by the group. She cared more about her horse than she did about people, and I understood this. She was twenty-one, and we shared the same room. She had a crush on one of the men there, and eventually she could stand it no longer and told me she was leaving and going back to London. I said that if she did, she would end up using. She asked me not to say anything about it till the morning, and I knew there was nothing I could do about it. She went back to London.

In the group, I explained why she had gone and that she would use, and I was attacked by people on all sides, who said, "How do you know she'll use?"

"I know she'll use," I said.

"You don't know until she actually does it."

But I was sure she would use, and I would have loved to have been wrong. She did use again and eventually died from an overdose.

I was moved into another room, which I shared with Emma from Bristol. She was extremely perceptive and a very gifted woman, but she couldn't stand me. She had a big problem even speaking to me. She was friendly with Theresa, one of the women I was supposed to be crazy about. Extended care was very difficult. I felt friendless, unsupported, and extremely isolated. I knew that it had to do with my sexuality. I knew also that if I had been a gay man and camped it up, it would have been all right. These women did not know how to relate to me, because I didn't flirt with them as they expected.

I spoke to Marilyn about the obsession I was supposed to have had about her and how I wanted it out of the way. In the group the next day, she said she was worried now that I would focus instead on Theresa. I was warned by one of the heads of the treatment center that if I caused anybody any unhappiness, I would be thrown out. I just couldn't believe this. Shusha was now in extended care and she was flirting like mad, but this was fine because she was heterosexual.

Christmas was approaching, and we were asked to prepare something for a Christmas celebration. It was suggested that I write some kind of skit, and I decided to call it *The Loo Ladies,* but I couldn't make it as light and humorous as people wanted. Tony, who had arrived in extended care, took over and wrote a very skilled piece based on Charles Dickens's *Christmas Carol.* He played Scrooge himself.

It showed a drunken Scrooge being confronted by people in the group at a medal ceremony.

We also went to the movies and down to the beach. I wrote a long letter to Pam and asked if I could see Maybe. She wrote back and told me I couldn't, that in fact she would take me to every court in England and Europe to obtain custody of Maybe because I had abused her. There was nothing I could do about this then, and I felt very guilty about my treatment of Maybe, so I let it go.

We had Christmas celebrations, but I could not be a part of them. On Boxing Day we went to an AA meeting in Bristol. At this meeting I said, "I feel like drinking. This is the flattest period in my life. I feel like I have no personality, all I have is my anger. Apart from that, I'm empty and miserable, and I didn't put the drugs and drink down to be like this."

On 27 December we started preparing for normality, the ordinary daily running of the place. On this day I gave out clean duvet covers. I never walked into anyone's room without knocking. I prided myself on my manners. I went around and knocked on the doors and asked, "Could I have the dirty covers, please?" I knocked on Theresa's door, heard her voice, and walked in. She was naked. I stood there, scarlet. One of the adverse effects of all those years on the streets was that if anybody looked at me too quickly, I jumped out of my skin and went red. I knew what she would think. I said, "I'm sorry."

"Get out!" she yelled. "You make me feel dirty. In the future, knock."

"I did knock," I said, and went to my bedroom, where Emma was.

Theresa walked in and said, "You make me feel so uncomfortable. Don't ever walk into my room again without knocking."

"I *did* knock," I insisted.

"You didn't," she said, and I knew there was no chance that anybody would believe me.

I went downstairs and had something to eat, and Steve, who knew me from the streets, said, "Chris, she's told everybody." I told him I hadn't done anything.

Then Marilyn said to me, "If you'd like to give me the house-keeping money, I'll check it."

"I don't want to give it to you. I'm quite capable of doing this job, thank you," and then I thought, *Fuck it! I'm taking that money and I'm going back to London and I'm going to drink.*

Soon I was back again on the familiar streets, renewing friend-ships with anyone who looked down and out. I woke up on the floor in someone's hotel room. I didn't know how I'd gotten there. I still had quite a bit of money left from the two hundred pounds of housekeeping money I had stolen. I left the hotel and booked my-self into a bed and breakfast in Paddington. Pam had given me Martina Navratilova's life story when I left the Ley Community, and I always kept it with me because I found it inspiring. I read it again in my room. When I went out into the streets, I couldn't remember where my hotel was; although I had the keys on me, there was no address. My mind had gone blank again with the drink. But the one thing I did remember was Broadway Lodge, so I rang them.

I spoke to Jessie, and she said, "You'd better send back the money that you stole from us."

"I have no money left and I don't feel guilty."

"Oh yeah, well get to a meeting and tell them that," she said.

Instead of going to a meeting that day, I went around the West End. I drank and bought some drugs, and by evening I remember speaking to an alcoholic. This man had a bushy beard, and he was friendly with a Chinese man who was selling heroin. There I was, right back in the thick of it. Two men came up and offered to put me up for the night. News certainly went around fast. I went home with them and woke up in bed with one of them. I knew we had had sex. I still had my whiskey, so I picked up the bottle and downed the lot, then left the place feeling disgusted with myself. I phoned Broadway Lodge again, and Jessie told me to get to a meeting.

I found a meeting of Narcotics Anonymous in Rathbone Place, which was specifically for newcomers to share their experiences. I stood at the back of the room and shared my experience of ripping off the money from Broadway Lodge and how I had ended up in

London again, sleeping with strangers, drinking, and taking drugs. And as I shared I sweated. People said I cried. I felt as if I were sweating blood, as though I were bleeding. I just thought, I've blown it. Everybody there, particularly the ones who had tried so often and failed, knew how I felt and they came up to me and were supportive. But I knew that no one could do it for me.

I kept going back to meetings, and I got a bed again in 4 Birkenhead Street, King's Cross. All the people who were there when I left, like Yvonne, were still there. As the days passed, I either slept all day or ended up in a pub. I met a man who planned a robbery and said I could go with him. I went to a meeting and told them that if I did this robbery, I could pay back the money I owed to Broadway Lodge and start my recovery again, but everyone just laughed at me. One woman came up to me and said, "If you put down the drink, you might start to think a bit straighter, Chris." It was simple but I needed to be told.

One night I was invited for a drink with some of the women at Birkenhead Street. I had just gotten back from a meeting, and I said, "No thank you," and I didn't go. I had never been able to say no to a drink before. My days began to consist of going to meetings, eating, and sleeping.

Another Friday night came, and I decided to get some wine, go to a meeting, and tell them how much I wanted recovery. I sat between two people I had known on the streets who were totally committed to recovery, and I felt ashamed and left. I went out again and began drinking.

I went to a pub in Kentish Town and heard that Michelle, my friend in Hackney, had been found dead in the toilets in Trafalgar Square with a syringe hanging from her vein. In the lining of her jacket were £1,500 and a toy gun. Her face and body were covered with bruises. One ampoule of biseptone had killed her. I had been about to call for her, as she lived up the road from the pub with her brother. When I heard of Michelle's death, I knew my days were numbered. I had given her her first injection of sulfate—her first mainline injection—and I knew her to be a survivor. Michelle was from Liverpool and she'd had it hard, but she'd also had a great spirit. She had been beaten as I had been, but she had died, and I was still alive. This had a profound effect on me.

The next day, a Saturday, I slept all day. On Sunday, 24 January 1987, I went to a meeting and said, "This is my first day clean and sober. I'd like another key ring." (Narcotics Anonymous gave out key rings to encourage people to work toward staying clean and sober on a daily basis.) Something had changed: I was truly ready now. It wasn't just about despair or running on fear anymore, it was the certain knowledge that I would die in active addiction unless I chose to recover.

I made the decision to recover and went to Dave, the probation officer who had secured a place for me at Broadway Lodge, that Monday. He said, "Chris, if you don't stop using, the drugs might not kill you. You seem to keep going, but the degradation, the way you are shaming yourself, will surely kill you." That made so much sense to me, and I told him about Michelle. He knew I wanted recovery, and he knew how hard it was to get through my first few days.

A woman named Lorraine said to me, "If you get seven days clean and sober, Chris, there is a group at the Chemical Dependency Center led by a counselor called 'Rock 'n' Roll Susie,' and if you go to that group, it will give you the support you need."

So there was my incentive. I got my first week and phoned Susie. She let me come to her group. "You're doing great," she told me, "you've got a week, you're on your way to recovery. Keep at it."

16

MY BEAUTIFUL LIFE

3 August 1995. This morning, as I walked to Wolvercote with the dogs, everyone who passed me greeted me. Usually I did the greeting, and sometimes I got acknowledgment; sometimes I didn't. In the end I got tired of this. I felt I was exposing myself too much, and I decided not to do it for a while. I felt good anyway when I got up, but I felt better when I was greeted. And I thought, Perhaps here there is another lesson, that instead of it being me that does the greeting, I should allow others the space to greet me. *Perhaps I had been trying too hard. My easing off makes way for others if they want to do it. So I am learning a great deal down on Port Meadow.*

After a very hard workout, which I enjoyed, I went to the health-food shop. Ruth, the woman who works there, has been very supportive

to me, and she has helped me to use vitamins wisely. She said to me to-
day, "Let me know when you get your degree, because I want to come
to the ceremony." I just laughed, and she said, "I mean it, Chris."
When I left the shop I felt an upsurge of emotion because this woman
really believes I will get my master's. I felt close to tears. It was the
kind of sincere validation that never fails to move me.

On the way to Robin's, my mind was filled with so many happen-
ings from the early years in recovery. One continuous thought was that
although my mother went blind, she had clearer sight than me because
I was blind until I put the drugs down. I know of a book called The
Veil of Addiction, *and I feel my veil has been lifted. Now I can see the*
beauty of life and can cope with those things that don't please me with-
out reacting out of fear or shame. My recovery is ongoing; it is the de-
velopment of life itself.

I joined a group at the Chemical Dependency Center in Earls
Court at 11 Redcliffe Gardens. I went there every week for eighteen
months unless I was ill. I also saw Susie as my personal counselor for
just over a year. I wanted so much to get a year clean and sober, and
she enabled me to do that. She suggested I go back to school and
set in motion the rebuilding of my life. Susie recommended some
courses to build up my discipline for learning. I booked courses in
creative writing, assertiveness training, and typewriting, all of which
I completed.

After I made my commitment to recovery, I was given a room in
the hostel of the single homeless project on King's Cross Road. I
had my own room there and no one to bother me. Here I could pray
without being watched. Praying gave me the strength to stay clean
and sober.

The first year of recovery was a long-term goal for me. Rock 'n'
Roll Susie said that if I paid back the money to Broadway Lodge, I
would feel better about myself. I got myself a little job cleaning
Susie's flat with a friend named Peter, who was also in recovery. The
money I earned was sent to Broadway Lodge. I didn't just pay it to
feel good about myself, but because I was going to be taken to court

if I didn't. There was, therefore, a practical and probationary reason, as well as the desire to make amends.

I also followed Susie's advice and got some voluntary work on the city farm in Kentish Town, working with animals. I went there three times a week. I loved animals and enjoyed working with them, but I was also a little scared—I had never done anything like this in my life, and I didn't know how to approach them. Because I had been taught to say a little prayer in the Fellowship to calm fear, I did this with the animals. I was told to take this enormous horse out of his stable and start grooming him, but he was kicking the stable door. How would I get the rope over his head? I took a deep breath and said this little prayer, and I managed to get the rope over the horse's head so he would come with me. He let me groom him without kicking me, and I was very pleased with this experience.

It was also suggested that I might like to ride him. He was the biggest horse of the lot and I thought, *Well, why not?* I had never ridden a horse. He was taken to the paddock, which was near the railway in Kentish Town, and although I thought he would be frightened by the sound of the trains, the animals were used to it. Once I was in the saddle, I felt I was born to it. I didn't know the right commands, but he let me lead him wherever I wanted to go. It was as though this horse knew what I was thinking. One of the women said, "Well, you look good in the saddle, Chris. You just need to learn a few things to make it a bit easier on your body."

The city farm was great fun. There were cows and goats. I watched these animals, and it was amazing to see how they played with their young and also how they allowed their young to play; they didn't bully or shout at them. I also watched the pigs. I had never particularly liked pigs and never knew why everyone was crazy about Miss Piggy—I actually thought she was rather revolting. Then something happened.

I became aware of the pigs watching me. They knew I was there; they didn't make any overtures or nudge me or anything, but just watched. I saw that they were very sensitive animals. So pigs and I became friends. Sometimes I touched them and sometimes they came up close to me and rubbed my legs. One day a sow was in heat. Her whole body was a pinkish red color, and she was really very uncomfortable. There was a group of women with a class of young children, and the women started squealing because the sow was getting overexcited. The children became frightened, and the pig ran amok. I grabbed hold of an iron barrow and called the pig, and she came over. I kept the barrow between us and spoke gently to her, and she calmed down. I felt she trusted me.

I loved working on the farm but found the work very tiring, which worried me. I spoke to Susie about this, and she pointed out that the young men who worked there had not spent a lifetime on the streets. I just needed to build up my stamina and strength slowly.

Every day I went to meetings and shared my experiences on the farm, which made people laugh. When I came home, I relaxed by playing classical music. My days were routine, but I needed this consistency. At the end of each day I just felt so pleased that I hadn't had a fix or a drink.

When spring came, I felt reawakened. Chris emerged. I was still the same person, but without the props and defenses that had hidden me. My senses came alive: I felt the breeze on my cheeks, I could taste my food, though I still smoked roll-ups, and I could really feel emotion. I spent time sitting in Regent's Park listening to all the sounds and gazing at the blue sky. It was such a very special spring, and the park was full of daffodils. I felt happy, clean, and sober. I was open to beauty everywhere. Even the color pink didn't bother me anymore, something that I had always seen as feminine in its worst sense. I saw it now in the sky, a mauve pink, and for me it was the color of love. I was still frightened walking down the streets, but I was told to greet people with a smile. I greeted everyone with a smile, and it seemed that almost everyone smiled back. I felt grateful.

One day I went in a café, and the Turkish man working behind the counter smiled. I said, "What are you laughing at?"

"Chris, you fill my heart when I see you," he said.

"Well, why are you laughing?"

"Because I don't want to cry."

"But why?"

"Because you're so happy to be alive," he replied.

During my creative writing course, one of the teachers wanted me to do a program for Channel 4 about my life, and I told him that I wasn't ready. He told me that I had something to offer the world and something to offer writing.

I said, "Well, I think I write like a sixteen-year-old, like a schoolgirl."

"Maybe that's where you need to begin," he said. "Nothing wrong with that."

In that class, I wrote lots of different pieces but found it difficult to complete any. One of the men got quite irritated with me and said, "Why don't you finish a piece of writing?"

"I'm trying out lots of different ways of telling stories," I began, and then I got stuck. I didn't know what else to say.

Bernard, the writing teacher, said, "And that's her answer." He understood what I was doing.

I started to do some service in the Fellowship. I did phone duty for eighteen months, which involved answering the phone to people seeking help, telling them where meetings were to be held, and taking messages. I would also tell them how to spot if they, their friends, or their family members were addicted. I stressed the personal choice involved in making a recovery.

On Tuesday evenings I went to a lesbian meeting inside the Fellowship. On 2 May 1987, just after a Bank Holiday, I felt a calling to Parliament Hill Fields. I lay in the sun near the women's pond all day. I looked at the sky and at the water where some of the women were swimming naked, and I felt safe enough to do so. I felt a part of, not apart from, my surroundings. As the day went on, I wondered why I was here: was it just for this realization or was it for something else? I kept thinking I'd see Maybe.

By 5:30 P.M. nothing had happened, so I went to get the bus to go to a meeting. Upstairs in the bus, I glanced out of the window and saw Maybe and Pam. I ran down and jumped off the bus. Maybe came over to me but Pam didn't really want to speak to me. "I've been waiting all day to say good-bye to Maybe," I said.

"How did you know I was coming?"

I told her I didn't know. "After this you will never see me again. I will never bother you again."

She walked away with Maybe, but then Maybe came over to me and we walked along together for a little while. She was a big, fat, old lady now. Gone was the street dog that she had been, the survivor and caretaker of Chris. I thanked her for her friendship and for helping me on my way to recovery, and then walked away. Back on the bus I punched the windows because of the pain I felt at losing Maybe. I had never had a friendship with any human being like I had had with Maybe.

I became a secretary in the Fellowship and led my first meeting. I seemed to have a flair for this role. I put people at ease and was able to be silly, even though I was very serious about my recovery. Many people came to my meeting. I took other meetings on Friday nights, and people came because they thought I shared in a wonderful way. I felt I was being of use. Here, the giggly side of me suddenly came to life—people liked it and giggled back, men, too, not just women.

My second year in recovery was similar, not as wonderful, but still about hard work doing the Steps. I learned to take care of myself on a practical basis, eating and sleeping sensibly. I read a book called *Mister God, This Is Anna,* about an abandoned child who was beaten up and adopted, but who had died at the age of eight. Anna knew God, and I felt just like Anna. I felt holy, but not because I went to church. Regent's Park was my church, nature was my God. In my mind, I used to see this radiant being like something from the films when I was a kid—Columbia Studios had a shining woman with all this light coming out from her. I decided that the image of an old man with a beard had to go, and instead I went to God the Mother.

I still had some anger and shame to deal with, so after my first year, I phoned my mother. I spoke to her, and it was as though all my resentment melted away. I heard the love in my mother's voice, and certainly I knew there was love in mine, although neither of us could say, "I love you"—it wasn't a language we used or had ever used.

Tina, a friend from the Fellowship, came with me to Bradford. I had believed all through my using, all through the time we had been apart, that my mother would not die until she saw me again. She was nearing eighty in June 1988. Tina and I traveled by coach and found the home for the elderly where my mother was staying, a more modern version of the Park on Rooley Lane. I was furious at Wendy and Trevor for dumping my mother in this place.

I walked into a large room full of elderly people, and I saw my mother and I knew her. I hadn't seen her for twenty-nine years. Her hair was short and iron gray, and her eyes were sightless—the cataracts were still there, they hadn't been removed. She looked older, but strong and sturdy. I went over to her and took her hand, and I said, "Hello, Mother." We didn't kiss.

"Oh, you got here then," she said, and we went upstairs to her room. I asked Tina to sit with us while I just listened to my mother speak. There were many accusations and some disparaging comments mixed up with confused recollection. The question, "Have you sown your wild oats?" was not one I could answer honestly, so I said I had, which seemed to satisfy her. I told her that I was going back to school to study. "Oh well, you always knew all the right people," she said, which I thought was quite ironic considering she had hated it when I had mixed with prostitutes and thieves.

I stayed about an hour, I listened, and I let her say whatever she wanted to say. She told me that my brother, Trevor, hated me and that Wendy didn't want to know anything about me. She had mentioned me, but they weren't interested. They had told her that if they arrived while I was visiting her, they would leave. "Well, I don't think I will be visiting you again," I said to her. "I will write to you or I can phone you, so that's not a problem. I won't drive Trevor and Wendy away."

She seemed okay about that, and then she talked about her wedding ring, which she said had been bought in Woolworth's by my stepfather. I asked her what she would like for her eightieth birthday, and she told me she would like a solid gold bracelet. "I don't think I can afford that," I told her.

"But you know all the right people."

"Even so, I don't have that kind of money. I will get you a present, but I don't think it will be a solid gold bracelet." I was very moved and touched by this, because my mother had never had a present of any value. She had always had cheap things, and I would have liked to be able to buy her the best gold bracelet, but I was never to give my mother the gold bracelet that she desired.

In recovery meetings I identified with other people; I learned how other people dealt with their daily problems and it helped me. When I saw myself in a shop window not under the influence of anything, I smiled at myself and thought, *I've done myself such a disservice.* I knew I wasn't beautiful, but that wasn't important anymore, and I didn't want curly hair anyway. What I saw was someone with something I liked, and it was a beginning.

I moved into my first flat in recovery, 66 The Combe, Roberts Street Estate, on the sixteenth floor, and I thought that this was a divine symbol, as I had come up from the gutter. I had a small balcony where I could look out at London, which at nighttime was very beautiful. I liked being high up. This was a one-bedroom flat with a large kitchen, hallway, bathroom, and toilet. I could not handle the comfort. I became aware of how limited my housekeeping skills were and realized I didn't have the creative ability to make this flat into a home. I was full of trepidation.

A day after I got the flat, I bought an eight-week-old dog on the Caledonian Road for fifty pounds. I called her Venus. She was a black lurcher with a white-whiskered face, and she was very frightened. A day later I got a pup I called Zeus, who had had six different homes. I let the dogs lie near me and they became friends. I used to get up at the crack of dawn and take my dogs to Regent's Park. My dogs became more trusting, and eventually people in Regent's Park would light up when Venus and Zeus arrived. Zeus was always extremely dependent; Venus was very independent, but she knew that I was her friend. The dogs and I were welcomed into this particular group that I used to call "the people of the park." It was quite a large group.

I used to call one woman in the group "the wolf woman," because she had a great kinship with wolves. She had lived with wolves, made programs on the radio about wolves, and sometimes when I looked at her she even looked like one. She introduced me to Daisy, a wolf in the zoo.

Daisy was the outcast of the pack. She had been reared by hand when she was six months old. Now she was rejected by her mother, who was the leader of the pack, and she was given a foster parent who felt unhappy about this situation. Everybody picked on Daisy. If Daisy had attempted to defend herself, the pack would have torn her to pieces. I saw the bites on her haunches and I used to flinch. "Leave her alone," I shouted. Eventually Daisy was separated from the pack, and for a while she grew in confidence. She walked with a lovely dignity and swung her tail instead of dragging it down. Then one day the gate between the two cages was opened, but not enough time had been allowed to elapse for the wolves. One morning Daisy was found minus her tail; it had been bitten clean through. It was decided that a wolf with no tail was no attraction for a zoo, and Daisy was given a lethal injection. The people of the park, including myself, were very upset. I identified with Daisy even down to the syringe that killed her. Like myself, she had been made a scapegoat.

As my life became more ordered, I needed to be informed about the world in which I lived—the drug world was a different world. I rediscovered my early love for learning. In September 1989, when I was two years and eight months clean and sober, I began an open access course at the City Lit in Stukely Street just off Drury Lane. For ten months I studied English literature, math, sociology, history, and study skills. I turned up every day, and I really engaged with the course, which irritated some people. Gradually, I began to develop a more disciplined approach to thinking, working things out, and writing essays. Then a wonderful word entered my vocabulary and my consciousness in a totally different way—*feminism*. I started to know more about what this really meant.

One of the women I read about was Sojourner Truth, a feminist and former black slave. Big and strong, she had worked on plantations in America and had been subject to whippings. She lost her children to slavery. Eventually she was freed from slavery and became a Christian. She became part of the evangelist movement in America and found an ability to speak out politically for black women. People listened to her. At one gathering in America, where she was speaking, certain men suggested she was a man. She showed her breasts to the white men who had challenged her and said that the shame for doing so was theirs, not hers. Her famous statement, "Aren't I a woman?" was coined when some white women were talking about how they were helped down from carriages and what great respect they were given. Sojourner Truth said, "Nobody ever helps me into carriages, or over mud puddles, or gives me any best place, and aren't I a woman?" This was one of the most courageous women I had ever read about, and she inspired me.

There were many experiences of this nature at the City Lit, and I was like a wide-eyed child. I learned halfway through the course that I didn't have to pass or fail, I merely had to complete the course, but this did not dampen my determination to do well. I was told that I could go on and do a bachelor's degree. I was speechless. Everyone encouraged me to apply, and although I found the forms an ordeal, I eventually decided to attend the University of North London, which was then the Polytechnic of North London, in the fall.

Meanwhile, I went to the humanities department in Kentish Town for an open day. I heard a woman named Lucy Bland speak, and when I spoke to her afterward, she said that she would accept me on the women's studies course unconditionally. I was just bowled over, and I knew that this was the place for me to go.

I had an interview with a man called Trevor, who I think is a professor now, and we got on well, although we were both nervous. He loved English literature and gave me a piece to read by Oscar Wilde. He asked me to say what I could read in this short piece and I did. I then had a formal interview with Lucy Bland. She just asked me to tell her about myself.

"We would like you to come on our course," she said.

"Does that mean that I am accepted?"

"I told you before that I had accepted you unconditionally, Chris, and I'm telling you now you're accepted."

17

"I LIKE WHAT I SEE"

4 August 1995. When I woke up today I was tired. Reliving my experiences is taking its toll. Even so, I have developed some discipline. I walked my dogs to Wolvercote, and this morning the breeze was fresh. The water was sparkling and wind rippled the surface of the water. What struck me in particular was the meandering of the river. As I walked, I watched the curving and twisting, and my thoughts meandered, backward and forward, round and about. Some sparkled and some were dull, and I thought I could bring these thoughts together, almost as though the River Thames were telling me how to continue my story because I am tired.

For the open access course I had to do an individual project during the Easter holidays, but I didn't have a subject. I met an Irishman at an NA meeting who was interested in magic and had traveled the world. He told me about a place called Tory Island, which was off the coast of Donegal, and I was captivated. It had a powerful history, so I started reading about Celtic mythology. I decided to go there.

I had never flown before, and I was so excited I told everyone in the plane. It was wonderful to fly above the clouds, and it seemed as though I could walk on them. After arriving in Dublin I set off for Letterkenny, and by late evening I arrived in Bunbeg, the nearest mainland town to Tory Island. After making some inquiries about getting to Tory Island, I met a sailor who said, "Oh, you're the English student, are you, who wants to go to Tory Island in the middle of the night. We won't be going tonight and you can't stay here, but there's a bed and breakfast down the road." He was amused that I was a student at such an age. I stayed at the bed and breakfast, which was owned by a friendly family who reduced the price from fifteen pounds to eleven pounds full board. The husband also arranged for a friend of his to take me to an AA meeting the next evening. Ireland was as friendly as I remembered it from my trip with Caroline.

Unfortunately, I was unable to get to Tory Island except by helicopter, and that was too expensive. However, the Irish Agency put me in touch with some islanders who were now living on the mainland. I met an extremely helpful man who was over eighty. He had lost his arm as a young boy by falling off a cliff while fishing. He explained that every family had a plot of land on Tory and every household owned a cow, a goat, and a horse. This simple way of living had survived despite the outside industrial world. Their religion was Roman Catholic but tinged with paganism. The ancient Celtic religion included a rune stone, and he told me the story of how the women had urged the King of Tory to turn the rune stone to save the men of Tory, who were to be taken away to fight for the British. The ship that came for them sank, and the men of Tory were saved. More than anything else the man seemed struck by the fact that after World War I women started to wear lipstick. He didn't like it; he told me he preferred his women plain.

Back in London my seminar was a great success. I included some music related to Tory Island and a video by the Irish musical group Clannad. I wrote up my notes and completed a five-thousand-word essay. But the most special thing for me was the warmth and welcoming of the people in Ireland.

While I was staying at the single homeless project, I was invited by a friend to spend New Year's at a yoga center in Kent. The center was a beautiful fourteenth-century house, and the celebrations involved sacred dancing and lighted candles. This was a wonderful contrast to the drunken and boisterous behavior that would be going on around King's Cross. I was given lots of time by myself to relax at the center. Days had a simple order to them, and in the evenings some people drank, but they didn't get aggressive. On New Year's Eve I joined in the dance to say good-bye to the year. I felt good. At midnight, we opened our arms and welcomed the new year and lit candles.

During my stay I read a book called *Foundations at Findhorn* and found out about a woman named Eileen Caddy, who had felt that God had told her to go to Scotland and form a community. At first the soil had seemed too barren to yield growth, but with Eileen's guidance the land grew fertile. Eileen meditated and received messages from God, and Findhorn grew from a trailer and just six people into a vast community looking for spiritual fulfillment. I knew I had to go there. I wrote a letter and I was accepted for a week on reduced fees. I was very excited. I felt I was going out into the world to find my own experiences, not out of defiance, but out of exploration, excitement, and adventure.

I arrived in Dundee by coach and had a cup of tea in a café—it tasted like the tea I had drunk as a child. "Aye they don't have tea like this down south," the man in the café said to me. I had about six cups of tea while I waited for the bus to take me to Findhorn.

I was greeted warmly at Findhorn and shown to a bungalow on the grounds, which I was to share with two people from Germany, an American man who looked like Clark Kent, and a lovely young woman named Susan with a silly Yorkshire accent that I grew very fond of. She had worked with addicts in recovery. We all met up in a group, perhaps thirty of us, and introduced ourselves. I found, to my surprise, that I was the most honest person, and many people were amazed by my ability to talk openly about my life. In this group was a gorgeous woman named Marianne, a beautician from Germany who now lived in Sweden. First of all, she wanted to do my face with cream, so I was quite happy for that. She said she wasn't going to put on lots of makeup or anything, but she wanted to work with my skin, which she thought was very fine. From the first hours of my arrival I felt at ease.

On the first Monday morning I got up early. It was snowing and I walked down to the rugged seashore. The air was so clear. Then the snow stopped and the sun came out. It was as though someone had taken a duster and polished everything I was looking at. Everything was so vivid as I turned round and walked back up the slight hill, into the grounds, and up to the topsy-turvy chapel. I took off my coat and shoes in the outer part, then walked inside and sat down. The atmosphere was serene, and there was a candle that was always kept alight. I saw Eileen Caddy meditating. I did not join her but tried to copy her concentration. I took deep breaths that I had learned at the yoga center and felt uplifted. Then there was silence. I left after a while, but only after someone who had been there a bit longer than me got up to leave. Time at Findhorn lacked hurry, and a moment could go on forever. I felt as if I had been in the chapel half a day rather than fifteen minutes.

Part of the experience at Findhorn was work. Everything at Findhorn had a practical purpose. One day, I shoveled soil into a barrel and tipped it on to a pile to be used in the gardens. While I was doing this task, I thought back to the time in Borstal, when I had had to fill barrels with cinders dumped from a lorry, a seemingly useless and tedious job. But this day at Findhorn, I relived these experiences, and as I shifted the soil, the memory of working at Borstal lightened. I had not realized how strongly I had held locked inside me painful times in my past. Many experiences at Findhorn opened up new avenues into my self-awareness.

For some time, I worked in the laundry with a man who informed me he liked my vibes, he said I had good energy. An American woman working with us said she was pissed off because she had paid to come to Findhorn and here she was cleaning. I said she should have some gratitude and that she was learning a great deal here. But at least she was being honest about how she felt, which was important. Some people took to the experience at Findhorn and let themselves learn; others stayed closed to all that was going on.

We were taken one day by coach to a beautiful and sacred river. I walked by myself and found a little trickle of water over the steps that led to the main river. I spoke to this little trickle, the runt of the stream, and I encouraged it to keep trickling because eventually it would meet and become part of the mighty flow. I sat by this river and absorbed the beauty of raw nature around me and felt inspired. We were also told that we could make a wish down here, write it on a piece of paper, burn it, and let it go. I wished for a woman who led one of the groups at Findhorn to become interested in me, and it nearly came true: She became interested in me, but I lacked the confidence to carry it through.

Eileen Caddy spoke in front of us and told us how she spoke to God, and I knew she was telling the truth. She was a very practical and down-to-earth woman who seemed to have no reason to make it all up. She said that she couldn't write, but that the words for the book I had read were given to her, and then editors had pulled the book into shape. I felt envious and resentful of Eileen Caddy, and I wanted to know why. It was not that I didn't want her to have these experiences, but I was keen to have my own, and hers just sounded so wonderful. I could see the gaps in my own development. Again I wanted to be somewhere I wasn't, without being grateful for where I was at that moment.

Eileen still lived in a trailer, and she invited me in. I told her about my resentment, and she thanked me for coming and told me some of her own struggles. She shared some very personal and private things with me, and when I left she said, "Go in peace." When she said this, it wasn't trite. It was her way of saying I should let go of my resentment, and that she had forgiven me so I could forgive myself.

One evening we went into the round temple and did a great meditation there; we sat in silence and I had this experience of being enveloped in the color purple. Purple happens to be my very favorite color. I opened my eyes and I could see, and when I closed my eyes I was bathed in purple. I was quite amazed by this experience, and I had to go to my room and be quiet.

I began to read some of the work written by the Essenes. I was interested in much of what they said about embracing life, but confused when I read that homosexuality was not a way of taking responsibility for the future of the human race. Rather than push my mind, I played some lovely music I found, the Taizé chant *Ubi Caritas:* "Where there is love there is God." This now meant something to me other than mere religion. It meant, where there is warmth between people, there God is.

At the end of just a week at Findhorn, I felt as though I had done a lifetime's work. In the groups, people who found it hard to speak were given the talking stone to give them courage to communicate to others. Susan, who shared the bungalow with me, told me how much she loved me, and I knew this was an unconditional love. She brought tears to my eyes. Other people gave me a great deal of thank-yous and affirmations too. At the end of the meeting, the talking stone was given to Susan to take with her for the rest of her life because she had such difficulty articulating her feelings. Then we had our photograph taken as a group. I still have this photograph, and it's strange: I was told to go to the back of the group, and over my head was the "No Smoking" sign. Marianne said to me, "I noticed you were sent to the top of the class." I thought it was to be under this sign, but she said, "Oh no, Chris, you were top of the class."

I returned to London feeling enriched, and when the summer came I said good-bye to everyone at the City Lit who had been so supportive to me and had given me the confidence to embark on studying for a degree. When I got my reference at the end, every single tutor said that I was one of the most rewarding students to have had in their class because I engaged with the subject. No one before had ever said they were glad I was there, or that I raised the level of what went on in a group. In October 1990, I was due to start a B.A. honors degree at what was then the Polytechnic of North London.

In July, before I started the degree, I obtained some landscape gardening work at London Zoo. The woman who employed me knew about me and gave me some brilliant hints about applying for the job, advising me, "Never say what you can't do, always say what you can do." So I stressed my gardening experience in prison and at the drug rehabilitation center, rather than telling them what I didn't know.

I spent most of the time at the zoo working on my own, which I didn't mind. I would get up at five o'clock in the morning and take Venus and Zeus for a run in Regent's Park before the day heated up. The summer of 1990 was extremely hot. I worked all day, walking miles with heavy equipment and barrows. My first duty was to pick up all the mess that had been left the day before in my area. After a tea break I would dig, water, and clear off dead growth. I was given a piece of earth that hadn't been dug for years, and it took me a week to dig through and rake. I had other jobs, too, like watering the vast areas of flower beds around the animal cages.

During this time I got to know some of the chimps, and I used to watch the rhinos, which fascinated me. The male and female rhinos were kept separate until the female came into season. Then they were put together, and the male rhino just didn't know what to do. I suppose if they had gotten to know each other beforehand, it might have been easier. Everyone sat watching these two enormous beasts trying to mate. There was a man with a walkie-talkie, and every time it looked as if it might happen, he got excited and talked to people in the office. But the rhinos never did mate, which is not surprising with all the commotion going on around them.

After I had been at the zoo a few weeks I went to look at the gorillas, whom I had felt wary about. They were so big and powerful, and I watched their movements closely. They moved with surprising grace and were very lithe. There were two females, one male, and two little babies. One of the females was called Zaire. I was drawn to her initially because I heard over the loudspeaker that she had a food problem. I thought she was an addict, too, and I felt a connection. At the time I used to roll tobacco, and I had changed from Old Holborn to a Dutch brand. Zaire began to recognize the smell of my tobacco because I used to go over and watch her.

My relationship with Zaire began to change over a couple of weeks. She started poking pieces of straw through the cage, or a bit of stick, anything that was there, to let me know that she recognized me. I pushed these things back, and the keeper used to shout at me. Keepers become very possessive about the animals in their care, and this one keeper didn't like my friendship with Zaire. I explained that she was doing it to me, and he just told me not to encourage her and to stay away. But I could not. I liked her and she liked me. It didn't matter if there were hundreds of people around that cage, she would pick up the scent of my tobacco and look through the crowds. Her eyes would look into mine with such tenderness. I thought I might be imagining things, but people used to comment upon it and say that she looked at me with love in her eyes.

The work left me feeling extremely tired, and I saw that some of the guys who worked there took lots of vitamins, mostly vitamins C and B, and iron. I took these, too, and went to my acupuncturist, who told me I was quite low on energy. I also contacted a healer, who took a lock of my hair. One evening, with Zeus and Venus lying on either side of me on the bed, I had a strange sensation that the healer was staring at me. The next day I phoned her. She had indeed been looking at me, by looking through the laser at my lock of hair, and I had picked up on that. She explained that some people were sensitive to such things. She told me that she didn't know what length of time I had given myself to heal, but I should multiply it by three. She could see the poor shape my body was in. She gave me some homeopathic tablets and advised me to build up my energy gradually and not to drive myself too hard.

I loved London Zoo and all the people coming in to visit the animals. I loved being involved. I had an interview with a public relations woman who wanted to increase the quantity of visitors. I said if they paid me, I'd help her because I had lots of ideas. But they didn't want to pay me outside of my job as a gardener. They wanted me to give my ideas freely, and for once I refused, thinking no, these top executives with beautiful cars and clothes weren't even willing to give me a small opening of just fifty pounds extra a week. So I kept my ideas to myself. Later, the zoo was working at a loss, so they wouldn't have lost anything by putting into practice some of my ideas. Despite this negative experience, the rest my time at the zoo was very rewarding.

My friendship with Zaire was very special, and before I left I went to tell her that I was going. I was sad to leave the zoo but returned there a week later with a party of people from NA. I revisited Zaire, and again she recognized me and everyone saw the special relationship there was between us.

After leaving the zoo I went to an organization for addicts called CORE, which stood for courage to change, order in life, re-entry into life, and experience of daily living. I did some voluntary work for them answering the phone, and I saw a counselor on a regular basis. I met Lady Diana Spencer, then the Princess of Wales, while I was lying on a bed receiving acupuncture treatment. I was glad to be lying down because in her high heels she was very tall, and I wanted to be able to look into her eyes.

"I've always wanted to look into your eyes," I told her. "I've read so much about you and seen so many photographs, but I've always wanted to look into your eyes."

She knew what I meant, and she said, "I like people to say what they mean."

"So do I," I said.

I asked her about the diaries that James Whitaker was writing about her sneaking out to the theater, pop concerts, and the ballet, but she wouldn't discuss this. She only said, "Yes, I do go to the ballet." I mentioned her children, and she became very gentle and held my hand. We had our photograph taken together, and I have kept it to this day. I told my mother over the phone about meeting Princess Diana, and she was quite pleased although she wouldn't admit it to me. My mother had always been a royalist.

I met a woman counselor at CORE who helped me get over some of the fear I was beginning to have about starting my degree. I had done all this dreaming, and now it was really going to happen. What if I wasn't as clever as I thought I was? I walked my dogs in the park even though my feet were still blistered and covered in corns from all the hard work at the zoo. Another healer told me that my feet were resisting change and they were a sign of an unwillingness to go forward. The future was scary even though it was so inviting. I was going to do my degree, something I had dreamed about all those years ago. Now it was really going to happen.

18

EMBRACING THE DREAM

8 August 1995. Today on my way to Robin's, I was stopped on the bus by a woman with her son, and she said quite excitedly, "I saw you on telly, didn't I?"

"You might have," I said. I spoke quietly because I didn't want everyone on the bus to look at me.

Then she whispered to me, "I was at the Ley Community too."

"How are you doing?" I asked.

"I've had a couple of relapses, but I'm doing okay."

I felt moved. People often come and greet me, particularly women, who saw the documentary Raising Lazarus *and watched me receive my degree at the awards ceremony. I think I speak to women in particular, especially those women with problems like chemical dependency, gay women, and mature women who think there is no possibility of do-ing anything different with their lives. I think the whole point of telling this story is to say, "I can do it and that means anyone can do it." The question always in my mind was,* What can I give the world? What have I to offer? *I had to move beyond the experience of living on the streets and the ever-decreasing circle of being an addict to become someone. These were some of the reasons I did my degree.*

I continued going to meetings and told everyone I met that I was going to do my degree. I already fantasized about wearing the cap and gown and shaking someone's hand on a red carpet. On 4 October 1990, I arrived at the Polytechnic of North London. A couple of days earlier, I had enrolled and had my photograph taken to become a member of the National Union of Students. I had never been a member of a union and I felt very important. I didn't go to the freshmen's fair, I was too excited and felt I couldn't cope, but I got to know all the different places in the faculty of humanities in Kentish Town. I met the people in the administration office, Jenny Dale and Sheila McElliglot; they gave me great support throughout my degree, and we are still friends.

I also made friends with Milton, who worked in the audiovisual department. We became table tennis partners and played every day. Milton was a black man, and I was a middle-aged white woman, and he knew that young fellows who came in when we were playing would kind of smirk and look at their mates. Milton would just look at me and say, "Keep it on the table, Chris."

"What do you do if someone sees you and thinks, this black guy, I'm going to beat him?" I asked him once during a game.

He said, "I keep it on the table and play the game."

One time a guy came in from the pub and began winding me up, but I followed Milton's advice and ended up thrashing him at table tennis. I said to him, "I tell you what, let's see if you can play. We'll have the best of three. You're not going to let a woman beat you now, are you?" I really felt that he needed to be taught a lesson.

Milton laughed, and he came and shook my hand, saying, "You're learning, Chris."

My very first lecture was on, of all things, discourse. We went into a great lecture hall, and I heard words like *Ferdinand de Saussure* and *signs* and *difference* and *structuralism*. Nobody seemed to know what was going on, and I am not so sure I did either, but it gave my mind something to work on. Information technology and discourse were compulsory for the first semester. Then there was English literature and women's studies.

In one of my early women's studies classes we had a lecturer from New Zealand stand in at the last moment. She told us about New Zealand and the Maoris and the Queen of Tonga, and she talked about their *pegs*. It seemed so difficult for this woman to do the lecture, so I thought I would help her out, which was pretty arrogant of me, and I asked, "What is a *peg*? Do you mean a peg that you hang on a clothesline?" And everyone started laughing. It was horrible.

"*Peg*, you know, that grunts," she cried.

I said, "Oh, you mean a *pig*."

"It's the way I speak," she said. "I am from New Zealand." I wanted to disappear.

The first three months were very difficult; everything was so new. There were union meetings and people without jobs for lack of resources. I listened to Revolutionary Community Party (RCP) and the Socialist Workers' Party (SWP) speakers, and although I was interested in some of what they said, I didn't like their attitudes toward women. I decided to join a women's group at college, and we fought for the right for only women in the college to choose their women's officer, so that men from the other parties wouldn't take over. This became an ongoing battle. Although I was nervous, I got up and spoke. I was torn to pieces by the RCP and the SWP, and I became aware of the viciousness involved in politics. Nevertheless, other women heard me and it encouraged them to speak up too. I became a member of the mature students' union, and later I became the Regional London Officer, for which I hosted a conference before resigning due to increased work pressures.

I began to get on top of my work. I attended most of my lectures and seminars, I engaged with the politics in the women's group, and

I was a member of the lesbian and gay group. I had many straight and gay friends who were proud of who they were, unlike the dykes—including myself—I had met in prison or on the streets. In college, I was amazed to find tutors who stood up and owned their sexuality, and this was very reassuring to me. The Polytechnic of North London welcomed people who wanted to learn, particularly women and mature students. Although there was sexism and some resistance to feminist ideas, feminist perspectives were used in nearly every discipline, and this was very uplifting to me.

In women's studies in the first year, I was taught by Lucy Bland, who went on to become a doctor; Sue Lees, who later became a professor; and a New Zealand tutor, Brian Wood, who was a poet and a feminist and who organized poetry readings. I attended one and met Merle Collins, well known on the black poetry circuit. She read her poetry and I loved it. Then I discovered that she was Dr. Merle Collins, head of Caribbean studies. I was very impressed. I was very attracted to this woman, but I had learned to control these feelings and we became friends. I used her as a tutor. I joined her Caribbean studies class late in my degree, and I was the only white woman in the class.

I was employed as the money collector and bouncer for social events, and people knew that I didn't drink. I observed students getting really wrecked, pissed,* and stoned, and it was not a pretty sight. I saw very few people actually enjoying themselves.

The most significant event in the first year of my degree happened on 31 May 1991, when I just about felt that I was coping with the degree. I rang the home in Bradford and my mother wasn't there. I spoke to the staff at St. Luke's Hospital, and they said they had sent her back to the home where I had last seen her. I rang St. Luke's a second time and insisted that they tell me where my mother was. They contacted my sister, and then told me that my mother had died on 1 December 1990, and I had not been informed. I had sent my mother money and a letter for Christmas, but there had been no response and no one had written and thanked me. I had spoken to

---

* drunk

Wendy on the phone, but she hadn't told me anything about my mother. I got Wendy's phone number again from the home, and she was furious. She blamed Trevor, who said he wouldn't come to the funeral if he knew I was there. She told me not to blame our mother.

"Anyway, you had thirty years to see Mother," she said.

"Are you judging me?"

"I've got no feelings for you," she said and put the phone down.

I saw a counselor at college because I felt as though I had been physically hit. She arranged an extension so I could do the rest of my work. I then stopped smoking and took up weightlifting. I just felt so angry and full of remorse. During the summer I went to Brighton for a week and got someone to look after my dogs. I attended a spiritualist church several times, and I also saw a healer, who helped me speak to my mother and Jean. It was a strange time, and it was windy and wet. I saw a film called *Dances with Wolves,* which seemed the perfect thing to watch at that time, and I got through the week. I felt dislocated and alone. Perhaps I had finally known what it meant to have a mother, and now we were separated forever.

I went back to college in September 1991 and got on with my essays. I felt ruthlessly determined to get my degree now. I went weight training three times a week in Mornington Leisure Centre in Camden Town, and I engaged further in the women's groups, speaking out with much more conviction than I had before.

In women's studies, I had a new tutor named Dr. Helen Crowley, who was teaching theoretical perspectives on feminism. This covered women and work, women and family, women and professions, and it looked at the work of theorists. Dr. Crowley was also a sociologist. She said that feminism came out of sociology because women who looked at society realized how male-dominated it was. Dr. Crowley opened my eyes to a deeper understanding of feminism.

In the second year, I studied gender and sexuality, and I was appalled. I wrote an essay on sexual murder and did some intense research that nearly sent me crazy. I hated the way men in America and Britain who killed women became folk heroes, like the Yorkshire Ripper: I had read that at a Leeds football match, the fans were singing that he'd killed ten women, who would be the eleventh? I went on a march with women in London in support of African women against female circumcision, and we held a candlelight vigil. Alice Walker, an American writer, was there to speak out against female genital mutilation, and Sirangit Aluwahlia, who had been freed from imprisonment for killing her husband, was also present.

Later there was a meeting at the Institute of Contemporary Arts in the Mall. A white journalist apologized for white feminists, and this annoyed me. When the woman who was facilitating the debate asked if there were any questions, I put my hand up and said, "Look, okay, this woman journalist has apologized. They need money, let's get the bucket passed around. What can we do about being sorry? Let's get on with some action." The hall erupted and people stamped their feet and clapped.

In May 1992 I decided that I could no longer continue living at 66 The Combe. A boys' club costing over a million pounds had been opened for Asian boys, but no building for white youths had been set up and there was a great deal of racial tension in Roberts Street. This was exploited by the British Nationalist Party and the Socialist Workers' Party. There were many young children taking drugs, and they harassed my dogs. Two gay men told the children to leave a car alone, and the gay men were beaten up by the children's parents. One of the men ended up in the hospital. One evening some stoned youths were hanging over one of the doors, and a young lad caught me in the head with his foot. He was truly sorry and he apologized. I really wanted to put his head through that door, but I said, "It's all right. Don't ever do that again." I knew that I had to get away. I went to Women's Aid and eventually they found me a flat in Turnpike Lane.

At the end of the term, while walking my dogs, I slipped and broke my ankle. I had never broken a bone before. The doctor said it was stress related. The woman upstairs in the house where I lived couldn't stand my dogs, and I was told by the Housing Association I couldn't keep them. I contacted some kennels in Hertfordshire and took my dogs there to be rehoused. I knew I had done the right thing for them. The next day my plaster came off and I started to walk again.

I did my best with my studies, but I didn't think I would complete my degree. I went to an AA meeting, and a woman told me to go to an organization called WISH, which stood for Women in Special Hospitals and Secure Psychiatric Units.

WISH had an office near Holloway Road. Here I met Jennifer McCabe, the fund-raiser, and Prue Stevenson, the director. Jennifer is now the director and Prue has moved on. Jennifer thought that I deserved support, and they invited me to come on a weekly basis. They said they would help me to find a counselor who would give me the support I needed to get my degree, and they did. Her name was Felicity, and she liked working with older women. She was older herself, with teenage children, and I liked her straight away. I saw her every Tuesday. She just let me pour out all my negativity and doubts, and somehow she'd laugh. She didn't laugh at me, but at the absurdity of these fears, because, as she pointed out, I had come such a long way.

There is a feeling of a sob catching the back of my throat because, despite all the financial hardships, college is a wonderful life. People experiment with sex, politics, ideas. They dare to speak out and often fall flat on their face. I did several times. Some of the mature students who had never had the opportunity to be adolescent were able to let their hair down and just enjoy themselves. I got so much out of being there. I learned again the value, which I had already learned in recovery Fellowships, of the strength in numbers. A lone voice does not have the same impact as a group. There was that wonderful experience of walking into the canteen and hearing people say, "Hi, Chris." Everyone seemed to know me, but then I had made a great effort to greet people at college, and it was returned.

In the final year in women's studies we continued feminist perspectives, and it was a very difficult program. The concepts of equality versus difference and essentialism versus constructualism were discussed. There was in-depth and abstract research to do. Up to Christmas, we were constantly talked to about preparing a dissertation and encouraged to set it out and find a tutor to be our supervisor. We also had essays to write and exams to prepare for. The library seemed fuller, and there were not enough books.

By my third year, the Polytechnic had been given the status of a university, and so the dream I had as a child was going to be realized: I was going to graduate from a university. I was to get the legitimacy I so wanted. I wanted to be seen and heard respectfully, not as an object of pity on a city street. The letters *b* and *a* are the first two letters of the word *bastard*. As a graduate, B.A. means bachelor of arts. I could now eliminate the *bastard* from my consciousness and replace it with the words *bachelor of arts*. It meant becoming the best human being I could be, a quality person, not mediocre.

I spoke one day with Dr. Crowley about the theory of anomie, when people feel continual unrest or commit suicide because they feel they have no purpose in their lives. I was afraid of the emptiness I had known for most of my life; whether it was real or perceived didn't matter, and I didn't want to experience it again. What Dr. Crowley said to me prepared me: "When you leave college you will experience anomie, Chris, just be ready."

"Is there a way of counteracting that?" I said.

"I don't know, you might find a way."

At Christmas I sent a card to Sister Frances Dominica at All Saints Convent in Oxford, and she wrote back to me in January inviting me to stay. I had met her while staying at the Ley Community in those early days of recovery. From my first meeting with her, I knew that this was a woman with a strong will. She looked people straight in the eye and greeted them. I went to the guesthouse in All Saints to stay for a few days. I spoke to Sister Frances Dominica privately and told her it was lovely to stay in Oxford and in the convent. I also told her that I was frightened about what I was going to do when I finished the degree course, and I asked her if there was a possibility of working there. I said, remembering the advice from the woman who had helped me get the job at London Zoo, "I can work in a kitchen, I can answer the phone like I did in the rehab, I can clean but I don't really want to be a cleaner, I have done some gardening, I can paint. There are lots of things I can do." She said she would let me know.

I returned to London and the serious work began on my dissertation: "Forked Tongue or Justice Deferred: A Case Study of Gillian

Darnell." Gillian Darnell was one of four people mentioned in a Channel 4 documentary on alleged abuse in Ashworth Hospital. I went to visit WISH and learned about the Ashworth Hospital, one of three special hospitals in England. Three men and a woman were involved, and I was very interested in what had happened to the woman. Yet again, the woman had not truly been heard. During the time I was writing my dissertation, she attempted to hang herself and was left with severe brain damage. I wasn't permitted to see her, although people tried to arrange this. The more I read about this woman, the more I felt her frustration and hoped I could give her a voice through my dissertation.

In April 1993, I went to All Saints again to prepare for my dissertation. It was Easter time, and I met Sister Jean Davina, who was to be very supportive helping me obtain my degree. I began to set out my ideas, and at this point I first met Robin Waterfield, who had trained as a lay therapist. I went over to his house on the grounds of the convent and asked him for some information about the ideas surrounding madness. Robin helped me to develop a framework. I was dismayed to discover that madness had always been defined by men. It suddenly struck me how neatly this fitted into certain theories I had learned about in women's studies, and I saw how the concept of women's madness hadn't been seriously challenged.

The third year was a difficult time for me. I knew from my marks I would not get a first-class degree, but I might get a lower second, which didn't seem good enough. Then I realized that, okay, maybe my analytical work wasn't developed enough to gain me the grade I wanted, but my dissertation would be. I completed all my academic work.

In April I had been to the Housing Association and told them that I was probably leaving. There was a new woman there, and she said to me, "Do you know there is no reason why you can't have a dog?"

"Can't have a dog!" I said. "Do you mean my two dogs were put away unnecessarily?"

I rushed out and bought the newspaper. I phoned up many places, and by six o'clock that evening, I had a dog I called Dancer.

He was eight months old, a whippet crossed with a Pharaoh hound, very beautiful and very frightened. The man who sold me the dog said his name was Rambo, and I just thought, *how cruel.* I took him home and gradually we became friends. In May the convent offered me a job in the kitchen, which I accepted.

We both moved to the convent and lived in Kojo's Hut in the gardens, named after an African boy adopted by Sister Frances Dominica. It was a small, simple room, perfect for my studies.

On 14 June 1993, I started my first full-time job in thirty years, working in the kitchens at the convent, and I felt anxious. I returned to this kind of work with an attitude fostered in prison and Borstal. For a while I found it difficult to settle in to working in the kitchens. I had also become self-centered and was still in the business of shocking or impressing. Because a kitchen in a convent is not the same as college, it was not possible to throw ideas around and disagree with people intellectually without them taking offense. I was open about being a lesbian, and this being a Christian place, somebody said to me, "Do you have to talk about that?"

"What's wrong with it?" I said. "Don't you talk about your boyfriend? What's wrong with saying I'd like a woman lover?" However, there were always these discriminations. It was so important to me that I be accepted as Chris, and most of the time I was.

I was invited to eat with the sisters and I became close friends with many of them. I also made friends with many of the residents in St. John's Home, which was a place where people came to enjoy their last years on earth, mostly people from the clergy. I met Sister Pauline, in her nineties, who reminded me of a diamond because she always saw things so clearly, and Sister Dorothy Hilda, whom I had met when I was doing my Step Four, and who was the first nun to hug me. Sister Dorothy Hilda was hunched over and tiny like a dormouse, but she was an extremely powerful woman. Although no longer working, she still actively prayed and attended all the offices. I had never met anyone so grateful.

One month after arriving at All Saints, I became a Christian. Sister Frances Dominica had been in Australia, and when she came back I asked if she could arrange for me to be baptized. She asked me when, and I said tomorrow. I was baptized on 29 June 1993 by Sister Jean Davina. I was welcomed into the community as a Christian.

I began my work on my dissertation and Sister Jean Davina typed it out for me, and when I rewrote it she typed it again. Robin also loaned me books by Michel Paul Foucault and others. Jane, who worked in the Porch drop-in center on the convent grounds, listened to my ideas. I took my dissertation to Dr. Crowley, who rubbished it. She told me I was too cocky and that I needed to rearrange it. I just thought that I could never do the ten thousand words. I felt totally defeated.

I got back to All Saints, and Sister Jean Davina prayed for me. I spoke to Jane and Robin, and they all encouraged me to do it. I did rewrite my dissertation, and Sister Margaret took it to be bound and presented beautifully. I took my finished dissertation to London at the end of August. Later, Dr. Crowley, who is not very forthcoming with compliments, said that I had raised the level of my education with this dissertation, and that I would now get a 2:1, a top second-class degree. She said it was a great piece of work, and she was very impressed with my lucidity throughout.

Just before I went to stay at All Saints, I had met Caius Julyan, a man who worked as a freelance researcher and producer. He felt the time was right to make a documentary about my life and getting my degree.

I said to him, "What's in it for you?"

He laughed and said, "I want to be taken seriously, and you want to write and have people know about you. I can help you do that, and your story can help me be taken seriously." So I agreed. Caius was given the go-ahead by the British Broadcasting Corporation (BBC), and he took me back to Bradford to revisit my past.

First of all, we went to a hotel on Manningham Lane. That morning, when I took Dancer out, I remembered the tall, dark, derelict mill building with its enormous chimney, and it was like it was when I was a child, except now these buildings were empty and standing on wasteland. I went back to the unpleasant hotel, and again I could pick up the roughness of life in Bradford.

From the hotel we went to Tumbling Hill Street. The cobblestones, the pub on the corner, and the street sign remained, but the house where I lived, and all the houses in the street with their steep, sloping roofs and their smoking chimneys, had gone. Only the ruins of what we called "the buildings" and the air-raid shelters where we played as children remained. In place of the houses was a university, Bradford University. When I saw this I was filled with wonder. It filled the extent of the street and halfway up the next street, which used to be called Richmond Road. This was now a place of real learning, not just the schools that had once been there and had been burned down. It seemed to me that out of my dream as a child this building had appeared as if by magic, and it was always going to be there.

We visited Scholemoor Cemetery in Lidget Green, and I bought some flowers to lay on the grave of my stepfather. It was just a little square patch of untended land between two graves, and I realized that even in death, this man was unloved. My mother had been cremated and her ashes scattered in the cemetery, so after all, only my stepfather was buried in the four-plot family grave. No one had tended his grave. I laid the flowers and wrote, "I now release my hatred. Rest in Peace. Chris." I tried to find my angel with the beautiful face, but all the angels I saw had insipid faces. She was gone.

From Bradford we went to stay at Wensleydale. I enjoyed the keen Yorkshire air. A few days later Caius drove me to Linton Camp. The school buildings were still standing, but they, too, were derelict.

We returned to London, and I was invited to BBC Bristol to meet the producer, Peter Symes. A car was sent for me. There were other people now on this team, and one woman named Fran picked up on my story very clearly. She helped me structure the documentary. I was also told that I would be paid, and I was amazed. When they said a certain sum, I increased it because I knew that I needed money and had big debts, and they agreed. They also paid for an outfit and a new set of dentures for my award ceremony.

The award ceremony for the degree was held on 14 December 1993. The night before, I stayed at Caroline's in Hackney with Dancer. Caroline had two children now. In the morning I took a taxi to the Barbican, and the reality of getting my degree suddenly hit me. I had invited many people: Sister Jean Davina, Sister Frances Dominica, Sister Karen, friends in recovery, Jennifer McCabe, Caroline who was ill and had to leave early, and a woman, Lyn, I had known on the streets.

On arrival at the Barbican, I was greeted by the BBC crew and given a bunch of flowers by Fran. Tutors came and greeted me, and when they saw the cameras they laughed. Dr. Crowley and Dr. Bland arrived. Lucy Bland was now a doctor, so I congratulated her. As I was greeting them I introduced them to Caius, who I felt was quite dismissive, so I said, "Hang on a minute, a bit of respect, please. These are women's studies doctors." I then realized he was very stressed out, and he eventually greeted them.

Dr. Crowley said, "You've done it in style, you've brought the cameras with you, Chris."

I wanted the world to see all these doctors who were women. They had inspired me to think about becoming Dr. Chris and perhaps even a lecturer myself. They had given me the confidence to speak in front of people and see how others listened and engaged with what I had to say. My dream was not over, it was just beginning.

I got my cap and gown, and on the program I actually look a little pissed, but it was nervousness—I knocked my cap offside and it was too late to adjust when my name was read out. We went into the Barbican Hall and tremendous music was played. There was a procession of the vice president, and all the tutors in their caps and gowns took their places on the platform. In front of their seats was a red carpet. Lesley, a man I had known in college, was giving out the awards. He was leaving the university to go to Leeds.

We were all lined up and it was our time. I had always been unhappy with the name *Wilkinson*—especially all through my degree, because this was not the name I wanted to have a degree with—so I asked to have my name changed. I chose *Kitch,* a shortened version of my mother's maiden name, *Kitching,* deciding that this would honor my mother. I had been unable to make amends because she had died too soon.

They called out the name Chris Kitch. It was a tremendous

moment when I walked on to the red carpet. I felt so powerful. I knew the meaning of self-esteem.

Lesley shook my hand and said, "I've been hearing a lot about you."

"Well, I've been hearing a lot about you too," I replied. We'd actually been quite powerful enemies during the student occupation of the humanities faculty in Prince of Wales Road, and now I wished him luck at Leeds.

I left the Barbican Hall with the other students, and some tutors spoke to me and wished me well, as did the BBC crew. I went back to Caroline's house on my own and stayed the night. In the morning I left for Oxford with Dancer. I knew I wasn't saying good-bye to college; I would go back one day and become Dr. Chris. And everyone told me I could do it. This was the realization of a childhood dream, not just for the child, but honoring the child I had been and the woman I had become.

I was Chris. I was now Chris Kitch, B.A. Honors.

EPILOGUE

THE PRICELESS GIFT

It is a beautiful Saturday in Oxford, 12 August 1995. I took Dancer, Bella, and Bess out and we walked to Godstow nunnery, made famous by the fair Rosamund who stayed there. It is quite a long walk from where I live by the iron bridge on Port Meadow, past the pub called the Perch and over the other meadow and past Godstow village. Today I went into the ruins at Godstow. As I stepped inside I was met with a deep sense of peace. I used to get the same feeling of peace when I stepped over the road into Regent's Park. I discovered this building only yesterday. The busy and noisy road is only two hundred yards away, but in this semi-enclosed space was a stillness. If I had known that people had prayed here, I would have picked up that this was a holy place. I had the same feeling I had had in the past when I went into old places of worship like Westminster Abbey.

I walked back with the dogs and was amused to note that Bella, instead of squatting when she had to pee, lifted her leg like Bess. Bella always used to squat, quite ladylike in a doggy world, but now she had started to copy Bess, who in turned has copied Dancer. I suppose they are challenging the gender roles of the dog world. Now they are all lifting their legs.

On the other side of the river I was enthralled to see the wisdom of animals. The horses and cows were in the water, and you could hardly see the ducks. The horses started kicking the water and splashing about, and it was clear to see that they just wanted to get cool and wet. Then they galloped away and sat down. They didn't go crazy and play like they do normally; they went and sat in shady places.

The dogs ran because it wasn't yet hot. As the powerboats came down the river, waves hit the riverbanks, and the dogs were frightened and ducked back. It reminded me of what I had learned in recovery about the ripple effect. I thought, *My God! Is that the effect my recovery has, just passing through those powerful ripples?* But I hoped my recovery did not frighten people off.

Everyone seemed very friendly today; they wanted to talk and I wanted to be quiet, which is most unusual at the moment. However, I did greet people, because I think there is something very special in greeting others, and it is always a way of acknowledging my own existence.

We walked on past the river and over the bridge by the canal, and I saw all the boats where the dogs usually chase a cat and get me into trouble, but today they didn't. They were well behaved. We were out walking for just over three hours.

I left the dogs after eating a very light meal and walked over the meadow to where I had found a bicycle. I decided to ride this purple bicycle that had been there for over a week if no one had come to claim it. I hadn't ridden a bike for years. I was frightened of falling off. I could see that this bicycle had either been stolen or dumped, because someone had crashed and the mud guards were broken and one of the brakes didn't work. It was a woman's bike, and I got on and rode it about a hundred yards. I was very scared. At first I couldn't get the thing moving—it kept overbalancing—and then I was off. I realized that I had to steer it properly and decided I would come back later on and learn how to ride a bike again. I want to be able to do this before I learn to drive a car or drive a boat, though there is a possibility that the latter might be easier.

I left the river and came up to the convent, and in the grounds I passed Sister Pauline. I took hold of her hand, which was lovely and warm, and she nearly burst into tears.

"Do you know who I am?" I asked her.

"Yes, you are Chris."

And I said, "Who is Chris?"

"The woman with the dogs." Then she said, "I'm so low and depressed," and there were tears in her eyes.

I asked her why she was feeling so low and she said it was because she couldn't see and hear properly, so I said, "But you can think, you can speak, and you pray," to which she agreed. I told Sister Pauline that she was one of my special people and she chuckled, her spirits lifted briefly. Then she asked me to take her inside, and she did seem so very low.

I spoke to the Reverend Mother, who asked me where I had found her, because she had been disappearing all day. She said that Sister Pauline was disconsolate.

"Is she always like this?" I asked. "I don't know her to be like this continuously."

"She is some of the time," said the Reverend Mother.

"Maybe she is getting ready to depart," I said, and I felt very sad because I think there is something very special about Sister Pauline, and I would hate to have her die, not to be physically present when I visit.

I walked on to Robin's. On the way there I began to make some connections, one of which is my big frustration at never being totally accepted as a person in my own right. Again, I was trying to enter into something that it was impossible for me to become a part of. I did not want to be a sister in All Saints Convent. But I didn't like the feeling of exclusion that always seems to operate in these situations.

I saw that, as a child, I could never have been a part of the family, because part of me didn't want to be, and only on my mother's side was I connected by blood. My stepfather and I had no connection, we were just two human beings brought together in a situation that was none of our making. I began to realize that I didn't want to be part of that family, and I am happy now not to be a part of it.

I was an outsider. I was also an outsider in the smaller community of the sisters, with whom I spent a great deal of time—eating with them, sometimes going to offices, going to Eucharist, supported and being supported by them, but nevertheless apart from them. At one point I saw this as a form of rejection; now I know I am welcomed into that group as a friend, but I am not a member of that group as a serving sister.

As I thought of this, I thought also of the expression "the priceless gift." The priceless gift for me is the gift of life. I wasn't living when I was taking drugs. I was going through the motions. I was unaware. The priceless gift for me today is that I can be open and honest, can admit how much I love the beauty of nature—even its raw and cruel side—and can appreciate my growing ability to communicate in the human world. I once read Hermann Hesse's *The Glass Bead Game,* and the gift I wanted was the gift of communication, not just with animals, but with creation. I wanted to be able to communicate and it didn't matter if people thought I was crazy because the gift of communication breaks down all barriers.

I was very happy this morning and very happy when I got to All Saints, and again I recognized the great joy I feel in having the courage to travel through all those experiences to arrive at my degree ceremony. And now I have traveled further, soon I start work on my master's degree at Oxford Brookes University.

The priceless gift doesn't mean there was no cost involved—the cost of addiction is a staggering price—it means I can put no price on this gift. The priceless gift is the freedom to choose, the ability to be spontaneous, to celebrate life, because my story is one of celebration. There is no doubt in my mind that the journey I have traveled was a part of my destiny, and yes, to some extent there was a choice in it, although I did become powerless through my addiction to drugs. I do believe there is a disease of addiction. Because I was not at ease with myself, I took things which shifted my perceptions and changed the way I thought and felt. I wasn't happy to be with me. Today I am happy to be with me.

There are moments when I am very lonely, and that's all right. I have heard people say that once they have made contact with a Higher Power they have never been lonely again. I have to say that this is not my experience, and the more I communicate with people the less I find they understand where I am coming from. It is simply that some people have not journeyed to the depths where I have been. This is not to say I am placing myself above or below anybody. This is part of my gift, to accept the lengths to which I went to destroy myself while something within me was indestructible, and that something I believe to be my spirit. That spirit may have gone into hiding, but it is indestructible. I don't know how to give it abstract words, but certainly I cannot describe it. I suppose I could call it "the child that was denied" because there is often a great sense of fun and amusement within me, waiting to leap out. I want to embrace life and to connect with people again.

These great lessons I am learning at the moment are also tremendous strides forward in my recovery. The gift of life is about growing and developing, it's about taking risks, it's about adventure. I met a woman last night on Port Meadow who spoke to me about someone in her family who had been a heroin addict. She still sees heroin as the worst addiction and has now had a baby and is drug free. She talked to me and I kind of talked to her, and afterward I wished I hadn't. The questions she asked me were unrelated to the situation, and I could hear her bewilderment about a great many things.

I said to her simply, "Are you taking care of yourself?"

"Oh, yes," she said.

"How?"

She couldn't answer my question. She said to me as we walked to the gate in the dark meadow, "Will you be all right walking back?"

"Oh yes, my Higher Power watches out for me," I told her.

"Do you have a hot line to God, then?"

"No," I said, "just a deep trust that everything will be all right, and I have my three dogs to guard me." So she realized that I wasn't being trite, that actually I was being deeply sincere and I was doing her a service, because she was alone, frightened, and her dog was an old one.

I heard myself say, "No, just a deep trust," and I thought how pleased I am still to have this trust, because it has brought me through so many experiences since I have put the drugs down.

I have never been without a roof over my head since 24 January 1987, unless I wanted to sleep out. Nor have I ever gone hungry. I have always had access to some friends and some comfort, except for those moments when it was necessary to be alone with whatever it was that I was experiencing. I have received verbal respect, written respect, tremendous greeting. I feel welcomed into the human race. Somehow this means so much to me, this acknowledgment and this respect. On some level many people do not understand about the depths to which I went, but in some way they understand the tremendous effort to climb back up to a level where the air is clean and I can look people in the eye—a place where I can tell the truth and say, "This is who I am and this is what I did."

I have been on television programs and have spoken on the radio and in prisons. I have been to special hospitals, mental hospitals such as Rampton and Ashworth, and I hope to go to Broadmoor soon to speak to women. These are tremendous opportunities and a real affirmation of my experiences and how they can benefit others.

The high cost of addiction has been used to great advantage in the priceless gift of my life. It is by reaching out to others that I can learn to value those horrific experiences that have been so damaging to me. I have mixed with members of Parliament on a television program about drugs, although I didn't find them stimulating or of great interest—actually I thought they were unimaginative in their approach to fighting, as they called it, the drug battle.

Again, it is the opening up of so many things. I am healthy. Yes, I am tired at the moment, but I am fit and healthy. I can walk for miles. I have my dogs. I have lived in a convent. I have lived in a flat.

Now I live on a boat, and who knows where I will live in the future. So it goes on. I have traveled. I went to Ireland and I have been to France. Although I have put a lot of work into what I have done, it seems as though I haven't really done that much to get these results. I have been available and I have been willing to engage with what I wanted to do, and it seemed to open up for me, but not always immediately. I have just found out today that the amount of money that has been donated to me is just enough to pay for my master's degree with forty pounds to spare. I haven't checked out this year's prices, but it could be that the fees have been increased by forty pounds, I don't know. I just think that it is amazing that almost the exact amount has been donated. I still have to find the money to live on, but no doubt something will unfold and something will appear. Again this is the willingness to engage with whatever comes along and, if it works, stay with it for as long as it is of value to me—and then to move on.

I have a flair for being with different people: people in recovery, children, professional people, people still using drink and drugs. I need to develop and work on this in many areas because I thought for so many years that people hated me. I now discover that within me is an ability to befriend people and also to receive a response, although not every single time, because life doesn't work like that. But on the whole, I am drawn to the people who respond to me and to whom I respond, and so it goes on.

Last night I looked at the trees, the water, and the sky; the woman I spoke to last night said it was a harvest moon, this great ball of red in the sky, and I was filled with awe. Perhaps some people do take nature for granted, but my eyes have been covered for so long that now when I see this life I know that it is priceless—it cannot be bought.

During the telling of this story I have felt increasingly that I am dying and it has been quite frightening. At the same time, there have been other sensations, as though parts of me were awakening, parts of my personality that have never seen the light of day, parts that had formerly been stifled. I feel a great sadness as I draw to the close of this part of my life story, and at the same time there is something else within me.

Last night I had a dream. Jean comes to me in dreams; she visits me. She is different now. Her long hair, which once was short, hangs down. Her gracefulness when she moves is still breathtaking. She is ageless and still beautiful. There is no addiction hanging around her. She tells me that she is proud of me. I never saw her for nineteen years, until I told this story, and now she visits me on a nightly basis. She waves to me when she leaves and does not beckon me to follow. She dances in another sphere of being. Sometimes she dances with the wildness that she tried so hard to escape from; sometimes she dances to another refrain, just a lilt from a Billie Holiday song. And so we were, just the two of us, all for drugs, body and soul, and we thought we were for each other. We are free now, for I, too, am free, free to choose a different way of life. There is a sadness though: I have never met anyone quite like Jean, yet I am happy with that. Now she isn't shamed, named, or labeled. She can dance with her beautiful grace and I can continue on my journey.

17 August 1995. Today I am preparing for an event that takes place in six weeks' time, when I begin reading for my master's degree at Oxford Brookes University. In the meantime I will rest and read, I will prepare myself, because now I know the value of preparation. I will walk on Port Meadow as I did today with the dogs. Today the heat was burning but still there was a breeze which cooled me. And I thought of heat—the fire and the furnace and the purification of heat—and I actually do feel as if through the telling of the story there is a kind of purification taking place, the lifting of deep dark things that I no longer need to bury within my memory.

I played with the dogs on the meadow, but we were quiet. We lacked energy, all four of us: Bella, Bess, Dancer, and myself. Dancer stayed very close to me protectively. Bella kept watching me, and Bess, who never does what she is told, was obedient. I felt as though these dogs were watching over me today. And perhaps I do need it. I feel as if I have spent myself in the telling of this tale, this tale of a journey that is not over, a journey that has within it many journeys.

A journey that is only part of a much bigger journey. The next stage is to go to college and to develop myself even further. Every day is for me a day of learning. That is the gift I have been given, to open my eyes and my ears and to learn to use my mind. Physically I have been ill, I have had bronchitis and a sore throat. Now I feel not exactly energetic, but refreshed, ready to move on. I feel again a newness in me, almost like a coming to birth again, an awakening of another stage on the journey. The end of the story is but the beginning of the story. I feel it is an achievement, not only to have traveled through all those experiences, but to have related them to someone else to read, people I don't even know; to have that kind of trust is an achievement for me. Even to discover that someone might be interested in hearing this story, or might be able to use something from it, is a wonderful validation for me as a human being.

Today, as I sit in Robin's study in All Saints Convent grounds, I feel peaceful. I don't feel today that I am dying. I feel that I am beginning again, and who knows what the future will bring? Who knows what tomorrow will bring? I only know that I am committed to today.

About the Author

Brought up on the tough streets of Bradford, England, CHRIS
KITCH's early rebelliousness soon turned into self-destruction.
Eventually, after many years of rehabilitation and many false starts,
Kitch emerged from this twilight world to realize her dream. Today,
she is a postgraduate student at Oxford Brookes University, writer,
lecturer, and television pundit.